T0113921

Endorsements

"Because of my long relationship with Jim Durkin Jr., I don't need to read his manuscript before writing an endorsement. I have seen his heart, his passion, and his commitment to the Holy Spirit to understand that if he writes it, I had better sit down for a long and transforming read. That's exactly what I experienced as I read *Dying of Thirst on the Bank of the River*. One of my favorite quotes is 'Humility allows me to serve others. Truly listening to the heart of what another person is saying will enable us to serve them.' I intend to make this book mandatory reading for all of the River team! Jim Durkin is part prophet and part theologian. These are the thoughts and visions of a man on a journey with God. It's a breakout book for everyone tired of the Christian ghetto."

Rev. Richard G. Oliver, international apostolic
overseer, the River Revival Fellowship

"Any contractor will tell you the foundation upon which you build is critical! With an evident love for the reader and the church, Jim Durkin does a phenomenal job cutting through all the 'Christian' noise. He points us to the foundation upon which we are to build our lives and relationships. I can't recommend this book strongly enough to all Christians, whether they attend church services or not. Jim hits all the right chords that we so desperately need to hear."

Loren Rosser, producer and
director of the Life in the New Covenant video series

"I especially enjoyed the chapters on 'Reality' and 'It Is Written.' The travelogue narrative sort of storytelling made it a very engaging read."

Dr. Stephen Crosby, founder of Stephanos Ministries,
Bronze Telly Award winner for the Life in the New
Covenant video series, and author of fourteen books

"I have often said that because of how we train leaders in the local church, these leaders tend to 'overlead' and 'overfeed.' Jim's journey in this book finally challenges the core issues for the life of a disciple: self-government and personal responsibility. This is not an attempt of a novice who just wants to bash the church. Jim is a father and a deep well of truth and liberty. Kudos, Jim, for taking us past the crippled concept of control as leaders to the freedom of personal discipleship."

Gary Goodell, founder of Third Day Churches International,
author of *Permission Granted to Do Church Differently
in the 21st Century* and *Where Would Jesus Lead?*

"It is refreshing and encouraging to read testimonies and insights of a man who has passed through so many challenges and disappointments in the Christian journey and comes through spiritually stronger with deeper convictions for Christ and His one body. The "nones" and "dones" among believers today can be reassured that although they may have been disappointed by various Christian systems, God is still very much living and working. If you are being stirred by God to have genuine fellowship and relationship with Him and diverse believers, you will resonate with the light in this book. This is Jim's journey of arriving at God's *ekklesia!*"

Henry Hon, author of *One Ekklesia, One Truth,* and *One Life & Glory*

"As I read through this most intense series of personal discoveries uncovering the eternal plan and purpose of the Almighty as revealed in the 'Profound Mystery' (Ephesians 5:32 (NIV): 'This is a profound mystery—but I am talking about Christ and the ekklesia'; a.k.a. 'church'), I realized that Jim Durkin would not, and still cannot, settle for anything less than Jesus's explicit desire upon Peter's declarative revelation given by the Father. 'I will build my ECCLESIA and the Gates of Hades shall not prevail against it!' (Matthew 16:18).

"Trust me, you will not put this book down. It's real. You will repeatedly see yourself, your own quest, played out in each chapter … There's abundant, pure, living water in this well … It'll quench your thirst, but you'll want more, profoundly more. Thank you, Jim, for this refreshing drink in this dry land. We desperately need it!"

Doug Krieger, publisher, Tribnet Publications,
author of *So, You Want to Do Ekklesia?*

"If there was only one book available to every sincere Christian, *Dying of Thirst* is the one I would recommend. This inspired writing is not a how-to manual. It is a treasure of wisdom and rare insight birthed from the heart of a pioneer with fifty years of experience in devoting his life to the pursuit of God's purpose for His church. How do we become living stones fitted together to become the church that Christ alone can build? Must we all agree on doctrine in order to live in the unity without which we have no witness to the world? Do we proclaim that love is our highest priority yet insist that we must agree on methodology, procedure, etc. in order to work together? Or does true unity result from remaining in the reality of Christ's indwelling as we learn to see other people through spiritual eyes? These subjects and more are handled wisely and in an almost conversational style.

"Jim is transparent with the mistakes he has made and the misconceptions he has held in the many years he served as pastor of several churches and various ministries. His presentation in this book reveals a humble attitude and the thirsty heart of one who is still running hard after God. Every reader who approaches this book with the same disposition will discover a deep well of wisdom that can lead to transformation."

Dave Frederickson, author of *When the Church Leaves the Building*

DYING OF THIRST
On the Bank of the River

Jim Durkin Jr.

WESTBOW
PRESS®
A DIVISION OF THOMAS NELSON
& ZONDERVAN

WestBow Press books may be ordered through booksellers or by contacting:

WestBow Press
A Division of Thomas Nelson & Zondervan
1663 Liberty Drive
Bloomington, IN 47403
www.westbowpress.com
844-714-3454

Photos for front and back cover: Bob Doerr (Visionary Photographer).
Front and back cover design: John Durkin Globex Branding, http://globexbranding.com.

ISBN: 978-1-6642-5473-2 (sc)
ISBN: 978-1-6642-5475-6 (hc)
ISBN: 978-1-6642-5474-9 (e)

Library of Congress Control Number: 2022901456

Print information available on the last page.

WestBow Press rev. date: 01/21/2022

Books by Jim Durkin Jr.

- *Foundation of the Heart*

Foundation of The Heart is the workbook for a course offered by Riverbank Ministries Inc. This course is designed to introduce the body of Christ to the liberty that comes from changing your core heart beliefs to line up with the kingdom's message. If you would like information on how to schedule a weekend conference, email Jim at papadurkin@gmail.com.

Foundation of the Heart is the sole property of Jim Durkin and Riverbank Ministries Inc., 3122 T Street, Eureka, California, 95503.

Contents

Dedication

I have known many who function as senior leaders of a congregation. To that role, we give the title pastor. Some go so far as to include it as a part of their name. Pastor Jim or Pastor Durkin would be examples. I have also known men who, without the title, were actual pastors to God's children. It is to three pastors I dedicate this book.

Leroy Metzger, a gentle giant. I first met Leroy when my wife, young daughter, and I moved to San Diego in 1977. We had only been married a few years and were still navigating the waters of our life together. Leroy and his wife, Cindy, walked with us, giving us gentle guidance in living as husband, wife, and parents. Leroy loved life and the adventure of following wholeheartedly the Lord, whom he passionately loved. That passionate love for Jesus came out in every encounter I had with Leroy.

John Heredia (Johnny), spiritual wisdom extraordinaire. Around the time I met Leroy, I began hearing about Johnny and his wife, Lynn. They had just moved from San Diego to Portland, so I didn't get the opportunity to get to know them. Some men's testimony precedes them, and Johnny is one of those men. Later, when I did get to know him, I experienced firsthand the wisdom and the depth of understanding he had in the riches of the kingdom. There was never a time that our conversations didn't stretch me to dig deeper into the things of God.

Scott Snedeker, what a guy! I suspect there aren't enough spiritual adjectives to describe Scotty. Scott was the first person I met when I arrived home from Vietnam. Mom picked me up at the airport and took me to a Christian commune where she and Dad were ministering. Scott came over to the car to greet my mother, and she introduced us. I wish I could say we've had an excellent relationship for the past fifty years; that would not be accurate. Scott is a worshiper, and as much as his worship reveals a love for God, his life manifested his love for God's people. That love moved Scott to speak a hard and even confronting word when he felt it was needed. I did not always appreciate his style and therefore distanced myself. As Jesus began changing my heart, I began to see Scott and his lovely wife, Ellie, differently. It amazes me that changing your perspective allows you to see others clearly. I began to see that Scott has always been a pastor—one of the best examples of a pastor I have known.

All three of these men have finished their race; their legacy lives on in the lives of those they have touched. Thank you, Leroy, Johnny, and Scott. Until we meet again.

To my wife of forty-eight years, Celeste. This journey would have been far too challenging if you were not by my side. I am forever grateful for your faithfulness to walk with me with prayerful, loving support and the occasional questioning. With all my love, I love you!

Preface

I wrote this book for everyone who has grown weary of religion, empty traditions, and the endless pursuit of assuring that all our doctrines are more biblically correct than other churches'.

I struggled over how to approach the writing of this book. I know the Lord laid it on my heart to write. It was the *how* that became the struggle. I knew I didn't want to approach it as a how-to book. How much of my story am I willing to share? If I share too much of my journey, will the reader identify, or will it just come off as one man's story?

Over fifty years of ministry, I've possibly made every mistake that one can make. One thing I know is that in all of it, I never lost sight of two things. First, I do not want to misrepresent God. Second, I have a desire to help others live in the promises of the kingdom. This motivation has caused me to take on many tasks beyond my level of grace. The writing of this book, however, is not one of those endeavors.

I feel the grace of the Lord to write about my life story and the lessons learned. I have seen far too many believers struggling to get what they confess to believe working in their life. Peace and joy are too often circumstantial. Walking in the victory that comes immediately after a breakthrough, over time, reverts to previous norms. Others are endlessly pursuing experiences they equate with a fresh outpouring of the spirit, seeking the breakthrough that will rekindle their passion.

The pull to accept a norm that neither satisfies our thirst nor refreshes our soul remains. Endlessly hearing we are on the threshold of the greatest revival leaves one discouraged and incapable of hope for seeing promises fulfilled. The surrender is what I've identified as "dying of thirst on the bank of the river." I spent almost twenty years in that place—a place of serving a religious structure in the name of working for the master of that religion.

At the time, I believed I was serving the Lord, and I was. As I saw it, working for the Lord meant ensuring that the system was cutting edge, biblically sound, and appealing to the lost and had a message that both convicted and brought hope.

In all the activity, occasionally a feeling of dissatisfaction arose. Quick to put it in its place, behind the cross, I'd enter whatever spiritual practice worked to bring me out from under this attack. Doubt is not of God, or so we're taught. No thought that sounds like doubting our practices can be of God, right? Today I'd answer that with stating I don't believe it is doubt. Maybe thirst was revealing itself and all the religious practices are attempts to quench the thirst with bitter water.

The invitation was never to join a religion. The invitation was never about escaping a future judgment and penalty for a life of sin. The invitation is the same as it was for the woman at the well in Samaria. Jesus said, "Drink of the water that I give and never thirst again." The water Jesus gives is a growing, vital, and abiding relationship with the Father, the Son, and the Holy Spirit. This relationship will satisfy every desire on every level, every day, for the remainder of one's life.

Why is it that so few ever find that place? For the past twenty years, I have never stopped pursuing an answer to that question. Should it have to take that long to discover the answer? No, unless you are entrenched in religious traditions, beliefs, and practices. The saying goes that there is none so blind as he who will not see. Jesus told His disciples He spoke in parables because the kingdom's secrets were theirs to understand, but for the people, it was so that seeing they would not perceive and hearing they would not understand. That was me, and it represents so many I have met over my lifetime. I do not write this to shame anyone but to expose what religion has done to us all. Jesus came to set us free. Paul said, having been set free, do not return to the yoke of bondage. He was speaking of religious bondage.

In my twenty-year journey, I have asked the Lord hundreds of questions. I've been like the student who's constantly interrupting the teacher. Some of my friends, like fellow students, have gotten upset with me for continually questioning. "Jim, why don't you be quiet and accept what the teachers are saying? Why do you always have to disrupt the flow of things?"

One day as things began to change in my understanding, I asked the Lord why I saw these things when no one else I knew was. He said, "Because you asked." My encouragement to you is not to be afraid to be the one with questions. My journey has not been easy. I've been misunderstood, warned against, rejected, and judged to be in serious error. Because I no longer accept what my branch of religious affiliation declares to be correct doctrine and practice, some think I'm rebellious, antichurch, and walking in deception. None of which I believe to be accurate. Let me state with firm conviction I love the church. Jesus said He would build His church and the gates of Hades would not prevail against it. How can you be against the very thing Jesus said He would establish? In our current time, a growing number of people have identified as "dones." I spent a period identifying as one of them. I tried putting that label on myself, but it didn't fit. My love for the church that Jesus said He was building wouldn't allow me to settle for identifying with a label that brought even more separation. No, that identity seemed to be more bitter water that didn't satisfy.

Something about the abiding relationship in God drew me to want to have genuine relationships with fellow believers. I was seeking a relationship that was more than a weekly gathering. If it had to begin with attending a meeting, that was fine. If, while attending a meeting, I had to endure practices I no longer needed to refresh my thirst, was that a reason to cut myself off from those relationships? I concluded no. Relationships are too essential to separate me in my rightness. Isn't that what we've always done? Isn't that the very spirit behind denominationalism?

At the beginning of this journey, I suspect I was still under the belief that I was supposed to share all the wisdom I was receiving as the Lord began answering my questions. I was the ordained minister, and that's what we do. We give people answers. Over time I realized I was placing more trust in my teaching ability than the Holy Spirit's. Perhaps my only job is to help people understand that it's OK to ask questions, even ones that sound like doubt or questioning long-standing traditions and doctrines of the church. I now believe that the Holy Spirit really will guide us into all truth. In conversations with believers seeking understanding, the Holy Spirit often gives a deeper insight to us both. Through those who are not afraid of asking questions, the Holy Spirit speaks. Often wisdom comes through the weave of ongoing conversations.

In writing this book, I tried to avoid giving too many answers except as they came to me and for me. My goal has been to bring to light how easy it is to be drawn away from the flow of a continual abiding presence and relationship into accepting waters that never really satisfy the thirst of our souls. By sharing my journey, the process of returning to the river of God, and the lessons I learned, I hope to help the reader leave the waters of the tradition for the river of God's presence.

Acknowledgments

With the most profound appreciation and sincere gratitude, I want to introduce you to the people who have helped me on my life's journey. Through their influence, I discovered many of the lessons that have become the basis for this book. I am listing them in the order I was introduced to them.

- Jim Durkin Sr. 1925–1996, author, life coach, mentor, and apostolic overseer

  Jim Durkin Sr. was my father and the man who introduced me to Jesus. His understanding of the purpose and vision of God laid a foundation that has shaped my entire life journey. Dad walked with me in life until his homegoing. Dad, I love and miss you very much.

- Brennan Manning, 1934–2013, American author and public speaker

  I never had the chance to meet Brennan, but I discovered a love from God I never knew existed through his writings.

- Frank Viola, author, speaker, and blogger

  Through his books, Frank has helped me avoid many of the mistakes common to those searching for a more relational way to be the body of Christ together. He has also been instrumental in opening my heart to the joys of freedom from religious bondage. frankviola.com

- Dr. James B. Richards, author, life coach, consultant, teacher, and motivational trainer

  Jim may have had the most profound influence in my life. His understanding of the effects of heart beliefs, grace, and the gospel of peace has made a lasting impact. impactministries.com

- Wayne Jacobson, American author

  I can't say enough about the influence Wayne has been on my life. I have learned more about living in the Father's love and how to display that love toward the brethren through Wayne's influence. lifestream.org

- David Fredrickson, author, producer, and life coach

  David's love for the church and his desire to see it free from the bondage of religion continues to encourage as well as challenge me. familyroommedia.com

- Gary Goodell, author, itinerate coach, and mentor

  I don't know anyone who has opened my eyes to the way of Jesus in exercising leadership in the church more than Gary. thirddaychurches.com

- Gaylord Enns, author, public speaker, and mentor

  I wished everyone could know Gaylord. He not only writes and speaks about loving one another but also models it. loverevolutionnow.org

- Henry Hon, author and public speaker

  Henry has an understanding of the ekklesia that is so refreshing. I continue to grow in that understanding every time we talk with each other. onebody.life

- Andy Stanley, author, speaker, and pastor

  Andy has given me an entirely fresh perspective of the basis of our faith and the gospel. andystanley.com

1

Walk Away

ARE YOU DONE YET? HOW WOULD YOU ANSWER IF GOD WERE THE ONE asking the question?

Before I tell you how I responded, let me fill in the backstory. At the time, I had been ministering for more than thirty years. It was Sunday morning. I was at the pulpit, perhaps a half hour into my message, when I heard the Lord clearly say, "Are you done yet?" I looked down at another page and a half of notes and said, "Almost." I heard it again. "Are you done yet?" This time, there was heavy emphasis on the words *done* and *yet*. As I looked in my heart, I said, "Yes, I don't have any sermons left." "Then walk away."

Had I heard right? Had the Lord just told me to walk away? And from what was I being told to walk away?

I want to say right from the start that this is not a book about the shortcomings of the institution we call church. I will address many of the things I now consider to be less than what He intends for His children. I do so without an apology. This book explores what a vital personal relationship with Father, Son, and Holy Spirit looks like for the individual who embraces a Christ-centered community.

At the time, I was copastoring a small fellowship. Both of us had concluded that vast numbers of people had deep wounds from the church. We had decided that we wanted to reach out to the wounded in our community and bring them into a fellowship where they could heal. We spent nearly two years with an initial group of people who would later become our core team. We taught them how to relate as a family rather than a membership in an organization. We trained on the importance of and, therefore, how to hear the voice of the Lord and obey it. It is not only possible, but it is the heart of the Lord that each person learns how to be a healthy, spiritual, and mature individual while being a part of a community of believers. Our primary focus was teaching how to develop a healthy relationship with the Lord, discover our purpose in life, hear His voice clearly, and learn how to be a coequal and contributing part of a healing community.

How could it be that the Lord was asking me now to walk away? It didn't make sense, yet I knew I had heard clearly. I have never been in more turmoil in my life.

My childhood home was a Christian home. My parents were pastors, and all I knew was the life of a pastors' kid. Not to say that I didn't have some very personal and authentic encounters with God; I did. At the age of nine, I had an experience with Jesus I will never forget. At the end of the Sunday morning service, our pastor gave an invitation to surrender our lives to God's plan. I went to the front, knelt, and began to pray. I may have fallen asleep as sometime later, my father shook me and said it was time to go. In the time I was kneeling, I had a moving encounter with the Lord. He told me that He wanted to use me in the lives of other believers. He told me He would anoint my voice to bring healing. All I knew at the time, and the only way I could explain it, was I received a call to preach.

I attended church through my high school years. Frequently, I heard how no other denomination had it as "right" as we did. We were taught and therefore believed we had received the whole gospel and revelation of God. I had friends in other churches and came to understand that they heard the same thing about their denomination and that ours and all others were plain wrong when it came to certain things. That idea went so far as to conclude that certain denominations and groups believed in things that were so egregious that the deception they espoused would be the very thing that kept them out of heaven.

Upon graduating from high school, I left for Bible college. Away from home for the first time, I discovered life outside of the church world. My military draft number was low, so at eighteen, I enlisted in the US Marine Corps. In 1970, I had already spent eight months in Vietnam at the age of nineteen and was currently serving in Okinawa. I was mature, at least in my opinion, independent, and ready to take on the world. I had concluded that all the church stuff my parents raised me in was no longer relevant to my life. I was deeply conflicted. I was serving in the Marine Corps yet so desperately wanting to embrace the entire 1960s mindset and the experiences of my generation. Letters from home told me of a place that my mom and dad were ministering. As she put it, it was kind of like a live-in Bible college for ex-hippies.

Having been raised by these Pentecostal, straight-as-they-come pastors, I knew what a Bible school meant. Each man would be wearing a suit, white shirt, and tie. His hair would be neatly trimmed, making sure the length didn't touch the collar of his shirt. The women would be wearing modest, nonrevealing dresses. They would have waist-long hair and no makeup. There was absolutely no way that any hippie, ex or otherwise, would have anything to do with my parents, especially my dad.

When I returned home, I was thoroughly surprised by what I encountered: something I never thought would happen in this lifetime. My parents were involved with a Christian commune with thirty-five to forty young people. Men with long hair and beards, many with no shoes or sandals but wearing jeans. Most women had long skirts, and those who wore shoes had on sandals or combat boots. Once perhaps living as hippies, they now chose to live as Christians. In communes throughout Northern California, young people by the hundreds were finding Jesus and leaving the hippie culture behind. They sought to live together as they discovered the extraordinary life of being a child of God who was loved passionately and intimately by God.

It didn't take long (about two days) before deciding that this is what I wanted. As I was only home on leave for a few short weeks, I returned to my base to finish my military service. Four months later, upon being discharged, I returned to this commune in Northern California. I found more than a hundred people now living together, experiencing this life of being loved by God. My parents and younger sister were living there as well.

Living loved was the very foundation of our newfound life in Christ. We didn't know much, but we did know that Jesus loved us, and in turn, we loved Him. That was enough. We wanted to share that simple message with everyone.

We soon began to think about taking this gospel message, the good news of God's love, into the world. Teams were formed and sent out to cities like New York, Chicago, San Francisco, and Los Angeles, to name a few. Germany, France, England, Italy, and Japan were other locations teams were sent to.

Is living loved enough? I don't know if anyone asked that question, but it seems like somewhere along the line, we answered it with a resounding no. No, you can't just live your Christian life receiving love from God and loving Him in return. It would be necessary to grow up into maturity as a believer. How to mature as a Christian must be taught. I am not suggesting that teaching in and of itself is wrong; I am saying that the way we approached it opened the door to return to the entrapment of religious bondage.

The apostle Paul in Galatians asks, "Who has bewitched you?" With the benefit of hindsight, I wonder how we allowed that of ourselves. In the beginning, we were encouraged to seek to know God. Learning His ways, His voice, and how He guided us as individual members of Christ's body. Over time, however, the teachings began to take on a subtle change. Those changes altered the foundation of Christ and transformed it into the foundation of the Christian life.

It was early on that balance was introduced. There was always someone who sought to bring every teaching into balance. Leaders taught against the "God and me syndrome." That is the belief that you could receive guidance directly from the Lord and following the Holy Spirit's direction would keep you safe. Instead, the teaching was that you had to be in a relationship with an entire community submitted to the covering of leadership. As created beings, we need the brethren, especially leaders, to keep us from going astray. It's the "iron sharpens iron" thing. Don't get me wrong here. I embrace the interdependence of Christ's body. I honor God-ordained leadership when it's functioning correctly within the body. I believe that we are individuals within the community. I'll share more on this in chapter 11.

The teaching at the time said it's in the multitude of counsel that we find wisdom and safety. That statement alone is not wrong. How can it be? It's a quote from King Solomon recorded in scripture. However, it was rare that the balance of *if a person lacked wisdom,* he or she should ask God, and He would give it liberally was offered. The result was most of us stopped turning to God for insight. We turned to others to tell us what they thought we should do. A belief prevailed that certain men discerned the mind of God better than we did. They could bring forth the wisdom of God for any situation. We needed to submit to them and not rely on our judgment. These older brothers taught us that we could not trust the inner voice because the heart was deceitful and desperately wicked; therefore, we needed to submit every decision to the counsel of older brethren who knew the ways of God. At first, it seemed to be a good thing; the wisdom they shared with us kept us from making what could have been severe mistakes in some cases. Within a short period, older brothers became the voice of authority in every area of our lives.

When the discipleship/shepherding movement of the seventies and eighties came to the forefront of the Jesus People Movement, we accepted it without question. The abuses, various forms of manipulation, and control that people in churches experienced were magnified and multiplied in Christian communes. By way of personal confession, just like the frog in the pot of water that will cook if you turn the heat on and bring the water to a boiling point, I gave in to the spirit of control degree by degree. First, others controlled me. Later, I became the controller as I became accepted as an older brother.

Perhaps one of the most significant downsides of a Christian community centered around strong or charismatic leadership is the group mindset. There is a subtle pressure to shape your thinking to line up with what comes from the person or persons who fill the pulpit. We form small group meetings to support the primary teaching. We design questions to be considered that focus your attention on the group's way of rightly dividing the word of truth. The new members soon discover how similar everyone's experiences are. They realize that everyone is on the same page when it comes to their beliefs. As a result, they begin to feel a subtle pressure for their journey to look the same. They seek to have the same experiences, same expressions, and same discoveries. Independent thinking becomes viewed as they just don't get it or—worse yet—rebellion. This form of peer pressure leaves little or no room for individual thought that challenges or goes against the acceptable interpretation of scripture, the tenants of faith, and the group's practices.

Let me share a few observations. This is true in communes, communities, and churches. Whenever leadership replaces an individual's responsibility to hear from God for themselves, abuses will take place. Once praying is replaced with giving counsel, it's only a matter of time before some form of manipulation occurs.

Human agenda is exceedingly tricky to unmask until, in most cases, it is too late. Let's say that the purpose of a community is to reach out to wounded people. Let's not qualify why a person might be hurt; we're just going to create a safe community for people to connect with God. We want people to find their way back to their first love. In the beginning, we all start on a level playing field. We all have wounds, and we're all excited about the journey we're on. We are enjoying the healing process, and we love hearing the discoveries of others in the community.

Over time we begin to see something happening. Certain people, maybe even ourselves, begin to "help" the newer members with their journey. It starts innocently enough with just a slight correction or an adjustment to align with the older person's way of thinking. Bit by bit, the person who sees themselves as helping begins to interject their insights, convictions, and counsel on others. One of the worst things that we can do, and many times do, is that those bits of counsel work and at least temporarily speed the healing or spiritual growth along. But at what cost? Often, because learning to remain an individual within a community is a process of trial and error, sometimes painful, usually slower than we wish, people can find solace in having someone guiding them along in the journey. Here's where replacing the guidance of the Holy Spirit with human wisdom can wreak havoc. We begin to substitute the understanding that we are each members of one another. Instead, we establish a leadership that will teach us all how to live.

Let's consider the possibility that a group of believers wants to stay away from the pitfalls of the more institutional or organized way of meeting together. They seek instead to form a more organic community. In considering what a Christian community might look like, a few concerns come up. How do we handle a situation where a member of the organization wants to share discoveries that they say come out of their journey but do not line up with scripture? How do you deal with a community member who has an obvious gift of leadership or a gift of teaching (Romans 12) and keeps trying to push that gift onto others? Suppose that the community is an open community (that is, new members are encouraged to join in) differing from a closed gathering. How do we keep our hearts open to where we are in the journey and allow ourselves to be sensitive to the process that new members are experiencing without fast-tracking them?

It seems these or other concerns very quickly become the focus of the original members. What is missing here is that this line of thinking sets the original group up as the guardians of the community. The pressure on these guardians is to take control. They are now the recognized leaders, and the structures that give way to hierarchy are in place.

If we do not learn from the mistakes of our past, we will repeat them. To continue to do things the same way but expect different results remains one definition of insanity. A verbal commitment to not allow something to happen without first changing our core heart belief is not enough to prevent the same mistakes from happening. I will write much more on this in future chapters.

This hierarchical structure is what was beginning to happen in our church, but was that bad? Decisions were needed. We needed programs to meet the needs of a growing congregation. Not everyone needed to be part of every conversation. The core team and perhaps a few others who had proven themselves mature could make the decisions. As for the church vision, the two copastors desired to start it, and they should set the direction. It all made sense.

Now the Lord was asking me to walk away. From what? The community we were building. The people who were beginning to trust again. If I walked out, what would that say about my belief in the community? Would that damage, confuse, or offend others? Was I being deceived? Was I even hearing the voice of the Lord? Yet I knew I was. But why? What possible good could it do?

The original question remained unanswered. Why was God asking me to walk away? And more importantly, from what exactly? We started our church with a vision to help people who were tired of religion and wanted to get back to an uncomplicated relationship with the Lord. That can't be what He was asking me to walk away from, was it? We had spent a great deal of time teaching people to hear from God for themselves. We were teaching them that they had an individual walk with the Lord and that it is OK to explore that individuality and the heart of God for each person. That there is a healthy way to explore their relationship as it fits within the whole community. Why would God ask me to walk away from that? Still, in a great deal of turmoil, I made up my mind to trust what I believed the Lord was asking of me. I stepped out of my comfort zone and even my human reasoning, feeling the Lord would make the why clear to me.

Two weeks later, we left the church I helped to start. Over the next six years, my wife and I were on a journey that yielded both pain and joy. For probably the first year to a year and a half, I could not shut off my mind. The questions swirled in my brain. Why couldn't I just sit in a church and enjoy the worship and message? Was I going insane? Yes, that question came up often. Another one that perhaps scared me more was this: am I being deceived? In the beginning, there were far more questions than answers. Eventually, we found freedom from religious bondage we never knew existed. I came to certain other conclusions. We have come to accept so many things as being about the kingdom of God when they are much more about building man's kingdom.

A lifetime of religious thinking and activity had to change in my way of thinking. Although not attending a corporate church gathering, I was never out of fellowship with other believers. It's just that the connections didn't look like what I considered the teaching of scripture required. I never had more chance encounters that led to tremendous and encouraging conversations. In the grocery store, at the gas pump, at the park, and it seemed almost everywhere we went we met someone we had attended church with in the past. Also, I became more intentional about getting together with others. In the beginning, with friends, we knew from various churches. Later with others we met who were on a similar journey. The first mindset I had to get past was that if I didn't go to a specific location at a specified time, I was out of fellowship, therefore violating the teachings of scripture.

Jesus said He would build His church and the gates of Hades would not be able to prevail against it. In his book *Finding Church,* Wayne Jacobsen asks, "How do you think Jesus is doing in building His Church?" What an intriguing question. Consider what much of the world considers to be the Christian church. A Western understanding of corporate structure with its CEO, CFO, department heads, flow charts, annual budgets, etc. has influenced much of the Christian church. Is this what Jesus intended? Is this the church He said He would build?

I read in scripture that through the church, the manifold wisdom of God will be seen and again that Christ is the head of the body, His church. Old Testament prophets spoke of the last days, referring to something quite glorious. The knowledge of the glory of the Lord covering the earth the way the water covers the sea. Or the mountain of the Lord's house established and all nations drawn to it. Is it our multimillion-dollar buildings that will cause the nations to flow to the Lord's house? I think not. I'm pretty sure the prophet isn't speaking about a building made with hands at all. Presently, the Christian church is the brunt of cruel mockery, fodder for the stand-up comedian, sitcoms, and late-night entertainment.

The spirit of competition has become so subtle that it has affected every area of church life, beginning at the earliest age with which child can memorize the most scriptures. There is nothing wrong with memorizing scripture, but scripture is to transform our lives. When it is set as a goal of accomplishment to be rewarded by simply learning the words, it loses its transformation effect. You see the spirit of competition in the congregation in things like the best greeter, the most anointed worship leader, and the best Sunday school teacher. The list goes on and on. A new believer comes into the local church and almost immediately feels the pressure to either enter the mix of finding what they can excel at or decide that they aren't as good as those already doing the stuff. Hence, they settle into the complacency of just attending church. In the end, you have a certain amount of people striving to be recognized, a few who seem to be willing to help wherever they're needed and don't need or seek recognition, and others who never really get involved in anything. They seem to be content to attend meetings, visit with the same few people they've gotten to know, and go on their merry way until the next meeting.

In the first thirty years of ministry, I never considered that congregational members sit for their entire lifetime forever the student. The leader has all the wisdom. I was the teacher; I heard from God; therefore, I had attained. Now not only was I not in that place of teaching, but I was also no longer even attending the meeting.

After the first year and a half, I begin asking in earnest. No longer just keeping the questions swirling around in my head, I began to inquire of the Lord. I knew very clearly *what* He was asking me to do, but the *why* escaped me. Eventually, it became clear. It was right there in my answer. "Yes, I don't have any sermons left in me." That's it; my life had become all about sermonizing. I was the man of wisdom, the man with the answer for everyone else. I could come up with a sermon with truly little if any preparation. I had perfected the art of preaching. Now the message became all about hearing His voice and learning to follow it. The questions were these: When did I spend enough time with Him to listen to what He was telling me? When did I hear and follow His guidance? Using words and crafting them into principles to live by to help others learn how they must live is what I've always done. I believed that I was OK if I was able to teach with conviction. The hypocrisy of it was startling.

One of the first questions I asked myself during this part of my journey is "Why, after almost thirty years of going to church and serving in every leadership capacity, am I so ill-equipped to hear God for myself?" The answer was hard to hear, and I wasn't comfortable with it at first. The clear majority of Christians I know, which was certainly true about me, had reduced the Christian life to one or two meetings a week. How we do church can get in the way of developing a close, personal, and intimate relationship with the Lord. I believed I had one, and I did everything one is supposed to do to have one. I read my Bible, spent time praying, went to church, and shared the gospel with people.

There it was. The words "walk away" were an invitation to leave what I had allowed becoming a substitute for a living, vital relationship with my Lord. It was an invitation to experience the community the Lord said He would build. Before I would be able to learn, I had to unlearn. I had no idea how much I needed to unlearn, but I finally knew that I was ready to begin the journey.

2

Internal Struggles

THE PROCESS OF UNLEARNING IS NOT EASY. IT IS PROBABLY THE HARDEST mental, emotional, and spiritual struggle I have ever gone through. The need to be right appears to be a stronghold in the heart of most people I know. When it comes to spiritual things, most seem to hold on to their positions even stronger. It never ceases to amaze me how often I've met people very young in their Christian walk telling me with conviction how things are. They can tell you all about what spiritual practices are biblical and which are not. They know all about the doctrines of eternal security, sanctification, spiritual influences, and warfare, even which position on end-time fulfillment is correct. More often than not, they have all the proper Christian lingo down, at least that which is appropriate according to their primary source of influence.

We should expect no other result in a society in which we have promoted lecture-style collegiate learning over personal and devotional learning at the feet of Jesus and through the Holy Spirit's guidance. I think that's why being asked to walk away was so difficult for me to grasp. I had now graduated from being a student to being a sort of master. For the remainder of my life, I was the teacher who would be the voice of biblical authority.

My parents' convictions shaped my doctrinal persuasion and understandings. Those convictions stayed with me through the first twenty-five or so years of ministry. Even though I tweaked it a bit to fit cultural relevance, the underlying doctrinal positions remained unchallenged and unchanged. I remember hearing my dad, on more than one occasion, tell the following story. He was not more than a few months old in the Lord. He went to his pastor with a question. In the Bible, he read a statement that seemed to imply a different position from what the denomination believed. His pastor's reply was something along the lines of "Stay away from scriptures like that. It'll just confuse you. That's not our belief."

What was my takeaway from hearing that story on more than a few occasions? We don't believe that. If it's in the Bible, maybe I should ask the Holy Spirit what it means. Holding on to preformed interpretations of scripture opens the door to judgment. Those who have a different understanding are wrong. The spirit of superiority is at work, believing that I am right. The result is separation.

I was the superior one with all knowledge. That's primarily why my journey has been so hard. I don't think that everyone needs to walk away from institutional gatherings to hear the voice of the Holy Spirit. For me, it may have been the only way. The lessons I learned came with a price, and I had to be willing to pay. That price might not have been so steep if I had been ready to surrender my will and my stubbornness much earlier in the process. I sometimes still have a struggle with letting go.

While serving as a copastor, I helped lead a weekend get-away retreat for twenty to twenty-five attendees each time. The two of us taught a seminar we wrote on the transformation of the heart. This seminar addressed the subject of the beliefs of our hearts and how they dictate what our life experiences would be. We taught on establishing heart beliefs and how to change ones that do not line up with God's word. Because I assisted in writing the seminar and shared in the teaching, I convinced myself that I had it all down. I was the authority, and because I could teach on the subject, I had retrained my heart to believe all the right things. I couldn't have been more wrong.

Sundays would come, and Sundays would go. Most Sundays, I would stay home because God had instructed me to "walk away." On occasion, my wife and I would look at each other, and one of us would say, "Do you want to go to church this morning?" There was always the question of *where* if we decided that we did want to go. More often than not, our experience was not good when we did visit somewhere. We couldn't help noticing how religious everything seemed to be, and not in a good way.

It wasn't long before the internal struggle began, in the form of some authentic and earnest questions. Was I backsliding or deceived, and was I becoming judgmental? Or was I going insane? Every one of these questions seemed to come up in my mind fairly often. Friends who had known me for years asked them as well. I didn't seem like the same person they knew. The person who was so committed to the ministry no longer attended church. Now even though I seemed to be more at peace, not always needing to be in teacher mode, I didn't seem to have that same drive I used to have.

Was I backsliding? What an interesting question, and how was I supposed to judge that? Backsliding, the action of relapsing into evil ways or error. What does backslide mean in the Bible? Backsliding is the act of falling away or committing apostasy. It is a term used within Christianity to describe a process by which an individual who has converted to Christianity reverts to preconversion habits or lapses or falls into sin when a person turns from God to pursue their desire. Wow. Apostasy. Is that what was happening? Was I committing apostasy? I knew I hadn't reverted to preconversion habits, and I had not fallen into sin, but had I turned from God to pursue my desire?

I'm well aware that some who have known me my entire adult life would say that I have struggled with a more rebellious nature. I don't think I have. I prefer to think of myself as refusing to accept the status quo and being willing to ask the questions others refuse to ask or choose to keep to themselves. Why not ask questions? Why go along with the status quo to not cause waves? However, I wasn't just asking questions; I was acting out, or so it seemed. I had abandoned a foundational religious belief. Whenever the doors are open, Christians, and especially leaders, are to be in church. Now on the most sacred of days, the Christians' New Testament Sabbath, I was staying home. Maybe I was backslidden, but I didn't feel like it. My time with the Lord most days was more substantial and more natural than before I stopped attending the weekly meeting. How could this be? In my time with the

Lord, I often saw things in scripture that I had never seen before. I saw new levels of freedom, peace, joy, and intimacy.

> James 3:17
> But the wisdom that is from above is first pure, then peaceable, gentle, willing to yield, full of mercy and good fruits, without partiality and without hypocrisy.

Am I deceived? How can I possibly be deceived when the insights line up both the written word and the lives of Jesus, the disciples, and Paul in particular? Besides, the more I began to meditate on these new insights, as I said previously, the more peace I seemed to have.

One of the first things I began to hear regarded the simplicity of the gospel. Why didn't I hear these things from other ministers? Maybe I was just going crazy. Was I insane? Is the gospel as simple as John 3:16 implies? "That whoever believes in Him will not perish but have everlasting life." We know that there are different levels of belief; for instance, we are told that the devils believe and tremble. Additionally we read that "faith without works is dead". Finally we read that many will say "Lord, Lord, we have done many mighty things in Your name". The Lord will reply; "Depart from me I never knew you. The Spirit just kept bringing me back to the simplicity of that scripture; "Whoever believes, will not perish."

I don't know what it does to your mind when you bring up all your pretraining and arguments regarding what is required to make it into heaven, only to have John 3:16 scream at you in reply. I'm not talking about one sitting or even one day but months on end. I couldn't get away from it. I tried to base my arguments on messages I'd preached in the past. The scriptures I used that seemed to imply something different from the simplicity of Jesus's answer fell silent to the resounding voice recorded in John.

In the middle of wrestling with this question, another question flooded my mind. When did the disciples become born again? We all know, and Jesus said, "You must be born again if you want to see the Kingdom of Heaven." It takes the cross, the death, burial, and resurrection to make being born again possible, doesn't it? So why was Jesus telling Nicodemus that he had to be born again a few years before the cross?

In reading Romans, we see a comparison between the first Adam and the second Adam. We all know that first Adam sinned, and as a result, judgment and death passed on to all men. What does the statement "just like" mean? Through the obedience of one man, second Adam justification, righteousness, and the gift of grace is given to as many as received it. What am I reading? Adam's sin resulted in death and judgment on all men? Is this really saying that Jesus's act of obedience resulted in justification, grace, and righteousness to all and all we have to do is believe it and receive it?

This line of thinking led me to relook at stories in the Bible, like the prodigal son and the woman taken in adultery. When do you suppose the Father forgave his wayward son? I now believe it was long before he saw him returning home and certainly before he got his well-rehearsed "sinners' prayer" out of his mouth. What about the woman taken in adultery? Didn't Jesus command her to go and stop sinning? I'm not so sure anymore. If Jesus indeed had the power to forgive sin, as He said to the paralyzed man, and if in speaking by the authority of the Father could say, "Neither do I condemn you," then perhaps His words were a proclamation of promise, not a command. Go and sin no more. In other words, "Go. You're free from your sin." Is this similar to healing a disabled person and saying go and limp no more? Whom the Son sets free (does not condemn) is free indeed. OK, so I'm probably not insane, but why don't more people see these things? Actually, at the time, my question was "Why isn't anyone I know seeing these things?"

As of the writing of this book, many more are beginning to ask similar questions. I am concerned that we don't get ahead of the Lord in coming up with our answers. There is tremendous pressure on people raised on the traditions of religion always to have an answer. The explanation and the ability to articulate it is the end goal of most ministers I know. For me, answers don't come quickly. Questions follow questions. Even the answers that come in tiny bits seem to generate more questions.

Have you ever questioned why did Jesus have to come to make the Father known? Didn't the patriarchs know the Father? David, the prophets, certainly they knew the Father. Jesus is so different from the image we have of the Father when reading the Old Testament, yet He said He only did what He saw the Father doing.

> John 1:14, 16–18
> And the Word became flesh and dwelt among us, and we beheld His glory, the glory as of the only begotten of the Father, full of grace and truth … And of His fullness we have all received, and grace for grace. For the law was given through Moses, but grace and truth came through Jesus Christ. No one has seen God at any time. The only begotten Son, who is in the bosom of the Father, He has declared Him.

Does the God we claim to know look like Jesus? Does Jesus look like the God we claim to know? They should. Jesus declared that He and the Father were one. He said to Thomas, "If you have seen me, you have seen the Father." How do we reconcile what we see in the Old Testament and specific passages in the New Testament, including the widely accepted interpretation of the book of revelation, with what we see in Jesus?

Dispensational interpretation believes that God, because He is God, manifests Himself differently in different dispensations. How does that fit with Jesus the same yesterday, today, and forever, or "I am the Lord God I change not." And again, in whom there is no variableness or shadow of turning?

The questions don't stop now. The more I open my heart to examine past teachings, the more questions I have. I'm beginning to be more comfortable with the internal struggle. I no longer feel like I need to repent for opening the door by asking the questions at all. If I did try to turn back, I would have difficulty returning to the religious practices that left me empty. No, I've gone too far. I no longer have the choice or the ability to shut my mind off and return to pat religious answers I once comfortably preached with great conviction.

Coleading the *Foundation of the Heart* weekend, I started believing that because I could teach it, I had it all down. I couldn't have been more wrong. The transformation of the heart is really about getting what, as Christians, we claim to believe actually to work in our lives. God intends that all the yes and amen promises become our daily reality. Wrestling with the bondage of religious tradition did have a hold on me but not nearly as strong as my own heart beliefs.

Scripture tells us to guard our hearts because out of them come the issues of life. In other words, the quality of life you live is the direct result of the beliefs you hold in your heart. Hearing that my own heart may be sabotaging my life is not an easy word, and most people ignore it. Our heart beliefs define our identity—not our God-given identity but our self-image. Self-image argues against our God-given identity even as we are making bold declarations with our mouths.

As I removed myself from all religious activity, I began to hear my thoughts. In the beginning, when I heard things that didn't line up with my spiritual training, I rebuked it. As I began to learn about the transformation of my heart, I realized these weren't random thoughts but beliefs held in a deep place in my heart. So many of them were contrary to what the word said about me. Now when reading a promise of scripture, instead of thinking about how I could share it with someone else, I pondered the reality of that promise. Was that my reality? Scripture tells us that through the promises, the exceeding great and precious promises, we become a partaker of His divine nature, escaping the corruption in the world through lust (Second Peter 1:4).

How was it possible that I had grown up in church and spent almost thirty years as a minister yet so very few of the promises seemed to be a living reality in my life. I had come to accept religious answers that were no longer sufficient to quiet the internal struggles. I've heard it said, "Whatever you attach to the words I am, you become." There are so many things I've attached to the words *I am* or *I am not*. Very few of those things are the promises in scripture. One of the first ones I realized I struggled with was I am not loved (by God). I wouldn't have said it that way. I would never have confessed that God didn't love me. It's just that I didn't feel loved. That's one of the religious answers that was no longer sufficient. You know the teaching that we don't live by feelings but live by faith. Interpretation: even if you don't feel loved at times, you have to accept it by faith. However, the actual internal struggle is that I never felt loved unless I was performing because of my low self-esteem. Without the opportunity to perform, I had nothing to rely on to give me the sense of being loved or accepted.

I had a choice to make. Was I going to find a way to quiet my insecurity, or was I going to persuade my heart to believe the promises of God? I chose the latter. At the time, I thought all would change through a one-time decision. It didn't come that way. Transformation of lifelong heart beliefs is a journey.

The desire to honestly know love brought up a new set of internal struggles. As a local congregational leader, I was able to fill my social quotient through meetings and church activities. Once I was no longer in a structured Christian environment where I was the leader, I found myself highly uncomfortable. The few social events I did attend were awkward at best. I would seek one or two people I knew and spend the entire time with them. The first couple of years, most Sundays, I wasn't in my comfort zone of being with people who looked to me for wisdom. I was alone with my questions. No, that wasn't right. Yes, I was still in the place of more questions than answers, but I wasn't alone. The one who promised never to leave me was right there with me. The one He promised would guide me into all truth was right there with me, teaching me and guiding me through the questions.

I can't tell you how many books I've read and messages I listened to since "walking away." If there was a book that seemed to address the subject of one of my questions, I read it. I know some might think that is dangerous or can lead to confusion. I have more trust in my relationship with the Holy Spirit. Earlier I said that I've become very comfortable with not knowing yet. I keep my heart in the place of searching until I feel the Holy Spirit begins to supply an answer. Sometimes the answer seems to be the complete picture. Sometimes it's just a snippet, and sometimes it's to set the question aside for a time.

Proverbs 1:20–21
Wisdom calls aloud outside; She raises her voice in the
open squares, She cries out in the chief concourses, At the
openings of the gates in the city She speaks her words.

One day while meditating on this scripture, I had this thought. If
she lifts her voice in various parts of the city and on different streets,
then I'm going to have to go down roads I've never explored to hear
wisdom. I've read whole books only to find one or two sentences buried
in the middle that I took away as the wisdom I needed.

Have you ever noticed that once you give yourself over to follow the
voice of the Shepherd, wherever He leads often takes you in a direction
you never suspected? Six years later, and just as abruptly as the Lord
said to walk away, He called me to return to a denominational church.
It was the same denomination my father and mother had functioned
in as ordained ministers. I had said I would never be involved with a
denominational church many years before, especially that one. What's
that saying? "Never say never." My wife and daughter had attended on
occasion for the worship, so I felt safe going for that. I was sure I didn't
want to stay for the message as I knew what they believed and could
quote their basic Sunday morning message. For a couple of weeks, that's
what we did; we sat on the back row so we could make a quick exit.
After a couple of weeks, we decided to stay for the message. Things were
different. The young pastor's message was other than what I expected.
He had something significant to say.

Over the next few weeks of sitting in the back row, just in case, I
listened intently. This pastor had been asking several of the same questions
I had been asking over the past six years. Bit by bit, he and I began to
develop a friendship and explore many of those questions. I began to
have a hope that a denominational church could put relationships above
positions and titles. Was it possible that relationships could become
strong enough to allow individual thoughts and beliefs within the
community? Could a community exist that allowed its members to
struggle, be weak, or have needs? Could we meet and embrace each
other as a family? Are we able to rejoice as others experience victories or

weep with them in their pain? Will we become a spiritual community that openly discusses the insights received from the Holy Spirit and the answers to the questions that freedom allows us to ask? After a few years, we felt we had gone as far as we could with the congregation and moved on to new assignments in the Lord.

In this return to the Sunday meeting structure, I realized my biggest fear and perhaps the most significant source of my internal struggle. The need to be needed. In the religious environment, I discovered that being sought for wisdom was how most leaders and I found validation. There was always a group of people ready and willing to listen to someone expound on Christian principles and practices. In the time I attended that church, I only spoke from the pulpit a few times. It wasn't about the sermon any longer, but the temptation to give in to the pride of being one of the ministers remained the same.

Something was different. I didn't live for the praise of those around me. I discovered that the hold of low self-esteem that held me in bondage to performance no longer controlled me. Now the stronger motivation was a desire to see a community that looked more like what I believed Jesus said He was building. Above all else, a family that loved each other and loved each other right where they were with whatever ideologies they had or doctrinal persuasions, or even opposing political leanings. I wanted to see and be a part of a community of love.

The answers that did come during those five years manifested in some very unusual times and ways. Sometimes it was in something someone said in passing. Occasionally, it was in recognizing the error of some songs that were more in line with denomination teaching than scripture. During this time, I learned to listen and observe, which probably kept me from being drawn back into my weakness of making it about me "God's man." I'm not saying I didn't struggle with those old desires. I did. But I had gone too far in seeing things differently to give place to that temptation.

I have to say I am so thankful for the friendship with the pastor of that fellowship. For a few years, we met every week. In the relationship that developed, we allowed room for any question. When either of us felt like we were being drawn away and back into religious thinking, the other was right there with that all too familiar question "Are you sure? That doesn't sound right to me."

In some ways, the internal struggles continue. They're different now. I'm OK with asking questions. I'm growing more and more comfortable with fellowship wherever I find it or in attending a Sunday gathering. My heart's transformation to believe the promises of God continues. The most profound internal struggle is to see the church Jesus said He would build.

3

I Have to Do Something

IT WASN'T UNTIL I WAS WELL INTO THE PROCESS OF UNLEARNING THAT I realized bits and pieces of this new understanding were given to me over my entire adult life through visions, dreams, impressions, and experiences I had with the Lord. The following was one of those experiences. It was a day like any other. I was sitting in my recliner and reading Galatians. I began to hear the words I was reading in a male voice. It was as if someone were in the room with me. What I heard wasn't a reciting of memorized verses; it was as if I heard it from the author as he was speaking it. The words had meaning and went deep into my heart. I had a fresh understanding of freedom and grace. Later, in reading Romans, Philippians, and Colossians, I saw it again. Grace! Freedom! Love and acceptance came later.

What do I do now? I didn't grow up with the message of grace as I was beginning to see it. If I start speaking about this level of freedom, I'll be inviting a ton of resistance, mostly from fellow ministers. What if you had an experience of Paul dictating to you the letter to the church at Galatia? I'll tell you what I did. I began speaking of the revelation everywhere I went.

I did receive some blowback, not as much as I expected but definitely from whom I expected. Fellow ministers said things like "If you keep telling people they're free, they'll end up going back to their sinful practices." I argued but inwardly questioned the same things. I grew up in a church environment that was strong on the holiness message. For those of you not familiar with the teachings of these denominations, in the 1950s and 1960s, it translated into more that you were not able to do than what you were able to do.

In our particular stream of the Jesus People Movement, discipleship was the primary message. I still believe in holiness and discipleship. Just not with the same emphasis.

Was Paul inspired by the Holy Spirit when he wrote, "There is a righteousness apart from the law?" I had spent most of my life so focused on the seventh chapter of Romans, trying to get over into chapter 8. You know the things I want to do I don't do, and the things I don't want to do I do because sin dwells in me. How do I get to where I walk in the spirit so there is no condemnation?

The Holy Spirit led me to repeatedly read the third, fourth, fifth, and sixth chapters of Romans. I think I spent a few years in those chapters. It was the fifth chapter of Romans though that stretched me. Look at what Paul has to say.

> Romans 5:12–19
> Therefore, just as through one man, sin entered the world, and death through sin, and thus death spread to all men because all sinned—(For until the law sin was in the world, but sin is not imputed when there is no law. Nevertheless, death reigned from Adam to Moses, even over those who had not sinned according to the likeness of the transgression of Adam, who is a type of Him who was to come.
> But the free gift is not like the offense. For if by the one man's offense many died, much more the grace of God and the gift by the grace of the one Man, Jesus Christ, abounded to many. And the gift is not like that which came through the one who sinned. For the judgment which came from one offense resulted in condemnation, but the free gift which came from many offenses resulted in justification. For if by the one man's offense death reigned through the one, much more those who receive

abundance of grace and of the gift of righteousness will reign in life through the One, Jesus Christ.) Therefore, as through one man's offense judgment came to all men, resulting in condemnation, even so through one Man's righteous act the free gift came to all men, resulting in justification of life. For as by one man's disobedience many were made sinners, so also by one Man's obedience many will be made righteous.

The apostle Paul's words were unfamiliar to my understanding. Phrases like "therefore" or "just as." The most challenging was; "but the free gift is not like the offense, and much more the grace of God and the gift by the grace of the one Man, Jesus Christ, abounded to many. Therefore as through one man's offense, judgment came to all men, resulting in condemnation. Even so, through one Man's righteous act, the free gift came to all men, resulting in justification of life." I had read these words many times but never heard them. These words never made an impact. In his first letter, John says the reason for writing is that we may not sin. Paul said something similar. "I am dead to sin and alive to God. How can I, being dead to sin, live any longer in it?"

John continues to say "whoever is born of God does not sin. For His seed is in him, and he cannot sin because he is born of God."

Living free of sin goes against a lifetime of teaching. I am, after all, just a "sinner saved by grace." I sin every day. That's why I need a Savior. As we taught it, the message of holiness and discipleship said I have to do something, not believe something, to overcome sin. Faith without works is dead. I didn't understand faith or the powerlessness of self-righteousness. Also, I wouldn't say I liked the idea that all my efforts and attempts to produce holiness or my idea of discipleship were empty works and religious performances. In Colossians, Paul said believers are powerless when it comes to resisting the lust of the flesh through human effort.

As I began to believe that I was loved, not just universally loved as in "For God so loved the world" but as an individual who God loved passionately and intimately. He thought about me when He wove me in my mother's womb. God incorporated into my makeup gifts that are part of His nature. In my brokenness, He sent the Holy Spirit to draw me to Himself so that He could reveal His love to and for me.

Growing up, the Song of Solomon was a taboo book. Young boys should not read that book as it has some pretty graphic stuff in it. Later as a young married man, I was told that I could read it to learn how to spice up my sex life. Really? Is that the purpose of that book? While reading it, I realized this is a love story between the King (Jesus) and His lover/bride (the church). As I continued reading, it became much more personal. The Shulamite woman was me. I saw several levels of emotional healing she experienced as she responded to His love. I related to the emotional damage she experienced from her family of origin. I recognized issues like low self-esteem, poor self-image, persecution complex, and fear of abandonment, to name a few. I discovered that her healing came as she responded to His love. She didn't have to do anything to be healed or get over it except receiving His love.

I've battled low self-esteem all my life. I was afraid to let anyone know how poorly I felt about myself. My go-to response was to keep busy doing the one thing I had become good at: church work. The more active I became, the more people acknowledged what I was doing. Comments like; "We couldn't have done it without you" sustained me for days. Anytime I was alone with my thoughts, I would sink into feelings of being insignificant. The advice I got most of the time is when these thoughts come, I need to do something. If I immerse myself in Bible study, prayer meetings, or other church activities, there won't be room for these apparent attacks and lies from the enemy. It's when I give place to those thoughts that I partner with the enemy. In my attempt to hold onto faith and act like I'm victorious over these thoughts, religious performance consumed my life.

For years this seemed like the everyday Christian life, especially for someone called to ministry. The downside, which I didn't see for the first couple of decades, was spiritual pride. I was doing so much for the kingdom. That's how I saw it, and we are to be busy working for God. Idle hands are the devil's workshop. The challenge was to understand that God loved me. It was that love that gave me an identity as the one upon whom He had set his affection. He wasn't asking me to do anything to build His kingdom and certainly not as a way to combat an emotional attack of the enemy. That would have made letting go of the need to do something much more manageable if that were the only reason I kept so busy. The more significant reason was a wrong understanding of faith without works or the works He prepared for us from the foundation of the world.

I read that the work of God was to believe in the one He sent. There it is again, which isn't a lot different from "whoever believes will not perish". Can it be that simple? The prophet Isaiah asks a question. "Who has believed our report, and to who has the arm of the Lord been revealed?" Believe it. That's all. Believe that I had been set free from the need for religious performance. Trust that grace is a gift, accept that grace teaches me how to say no to sin, and believe that His grace enables me to do what I never could in my strength. He loves me, and nothing more needs to be added to that statement. Not because I think or perform right or any other thing to earn that love. Challenges presented themselves to everything I believed and preached. The challenge that concerned me most wasn't so much my freedom. I was beginning to experience a revival in my spirit. I was worried about what it would do to congregations if people started believing this message. What would happen if people found freedom from the need for religious performance?

Warnings came that the things I was speaking were dangerous heresies. I wanted others to understand their freedom and the abundance of grace. We are beloved children of God. He has freely given us the kingdom. He has qualified us, seated us in heavenly places in Him, and given us better promises. My heart was alive. I was more excited than I had been in years.

I eventually concluded that maybe their time hadn't come. I couldn't find any other preachers majoring in either of these messages. Perhaps I was deceived, confused, or insane. I was so liberated by what I was seeing that I wanted everyone to hear the news. The more I looked into the message that His great love did it all and that He's not asking me to do anything except receive, the freer I became. Scripture tells us that our actual labor is to enter His rest.

Now any work I did began to come from an entirely different motivation. Works were no longer religious performances. It was simply sharing with others about the liberty I was discovering. Creating sermons about my fresh understanding of the New Covenant wasn't my driving force. Sharing was the opening up of what was happening on the inside, not the preaching of sermons.

There is a danger in sharing about grace and freedom, especially when you couple it with God's passionate, intimate love and acceptance, apart from works. The risk is that people might begin allowing things back into their lives that they would never permit as long as we teach the severity of God's wrath and impending judgment. I learned that a person only returns to the desires they hold onto deep in their heart. The sin management approach did not give a person the ability to deal with passion, just the practice. I had to be willing to walk with those I was in a relationship with as they processed this new freedom. I had to trust the Holy Spirit that He was well able to guide them into all truth and that the Lord was faithful to complete the good work he began in them.

Some of the freedoms that went beyond what I would have said a Christian should allow challenged me. I often thought I probably opened a spiritual Pandora's box. Over time, however, I began seeing something I would never have expected. Many of those expressing freedom began to share various ways the Holy Spirit took the desire away for the first time. They knew they were free and no longer had to hide passions and desires that tempted them. They knew those expressions didn't alter God's love, acceptance, and approval. Responding to that love, acceptance, and approval brought them to where they no longer needed or desired to continue in those ways.

As more ministers began seeing these same things in scripture, they also discovered how manipulating and controlling tactics were used to keep people in line. Sin management has been the church's goal for so long that, for many, it is the only thing they know. Those previously looked to for lectures on the necessity of vigilantly resisting sin were now speaking about being free from such religious practices.

I suspect a close second to sin management is what I began this chapter with, the sense that we all need to be busy doing the work of God. Isn't that what scripture teaches? That we are His workmanship created to do the things God had foreordained. How can we expect to spread the gospel, build the work of God, and evangelize the unreached peoples of the world if we don't stay busy working for God? Under this collective mindset of sin management and working for God, the obligation of obedience becomes the rule of the day. How did the invitation to become a son or daughter turn into a servant (slave) mentality?

A pastor I know tells the story of being invited to speak in a church. He spoke on being free from religious obligation. For example, he said something along the lines of "If you are the kind of person who is under the bondage of 'have to' Jesus wants to set you free. Examples might be you believe that you have to begin your day reading your Bible or else the whole day will go wrong." Then he suggested that if that was your "have to," stop reading the Bible. Allow God to show you that His love and acceptance are more than a response to your "have to." He gave a few other examples, but that one had the most significant impact. Unknowingly he had addressed an issue that was almost a mandatory practice of the entire congregation. Sometime later, they invited him back. They asked him to let them go back to reading their Bibles. Yes, they took him seriously. Many had stopped reading their Bibles. Rather than being a "have to," fellowshipping with God through the written word was now a heart's desire.

This story clearly illustrates what not only I but many others experienced. Whether it's a wrong passion being allowed or releasing a "have to" legalism was gone, just freedom remained. Many who expressed their freedom to manifest worldly traits or desires of the flesh to see if God would still love them found that receiving His love set them free even from the temptation. For the first time, they experienced absolute freedom. Not freedom to but release from bondage. Those who lived in the bondage of "have to" found the joys of "want to." That only comes from a relationship of being loved and valued.

I wished everyone who heard the message of the glorious liberty in Christ would find the joy of that freedom. Unfortunately, that wouldn't be an accurate statement. Some walked away angry, even bitter that they had given so much of themselves and their lives to serve something that wasn't the heart of the master. Others doubled down on the message of the severity of God and immediate retribution for transgressions. Those who walked away from the faith concerned me the most. Was it this message of freedom, or would they have walked away anyway? I tend to believe that some of them would have wearied from performance and religious obligation and given up. Equally as sad, however, are the ones who dutifully press on, burdened down under the weight of earning God's favor, looking forward to the day when they would shed this mortal body and enter the joy of the Lord.

I believe we should all be looking forward to that day but not as an escape plan from the weight of a life in God. As His children, God promises peace that passes understanding and unspeakable joy that comes from the Holy Ghost. An abundance of life, and a transformation from glory to glory, is promised to us—and so much more. Before you try to balance me in your mind, I'm way ahead of you. I'm well aware of Christ's statement that "in the world, you will suffer persecution" and that the world will hate you because they hated Him. None of those things have any ability to take away what belongs to the kingdom. These things have been given to us by the Father. All the promises that have been freely given to us so that we might become a partaker of His divine nature are ours now, not just when we get to heaven.

Finally, in writing about the need to do something, I want to address what I consider a huge mistake: the desire to get back to some idea of how the early Christians did it. In most instances, it centers around leaving the corporate gathering place and meeting in homes. As if somehow, because we can find references in the Bible to going from house to house or the church that met in the home, we're following the biblical pattern. The attempt to be biblically accurate is an example of the "I have to do something" mindset that controls the Christian religion. The idea that we have to do things the way they did in the Bible.

I find more than a few things wrong with this approach. First is the idea that if we simply leave the dedicated building to meet in homes, we are more biblical. The disciples and early believers continued going to the temple or synagogues, as was their custom. Paul, on some of his missionary journeys, taught in the synagogues. So yes, both things were happening.

> Acts 2:42, 46–47
> And they continued steadfast in the apostles' doctrine and fellowship, in the breaking of bread, and in prayers ... So continuing daily with one accord in the temple, and breaking bread from house to house they ate their food with gladness and simplicity of heart, praising God and having favor with all the people. And the Lord added to the church daily those who were being saved.

There are a few things I've come to believe as I read these passages. As I already mentioned, they continued daily with one accord in the temple and house to house. It's that term "house to house" that stands out to me. Both in the temple and homes don't seem to translate, leaving the corporate building to meet in a home. The idea that a small group of believers will form a house church isn't consistent with this thought. The idea here appears to be much more centered in the fellowship, breaking bread, and praying together. Additionally, "house to house" implies much more fluidity and probably spontaneity.

The idea of the house church as being more biblical has been around for a long time. I've been part of several myself. I've read dozens of books outlining the author's take on having successful and more biblical house churches. Buzz words like *organic* or *relational gatherings* get away from the idea that this is an institutional group meeting in a house. In far too many instances, however, they appear to have taken on all the attributes of the larger gatherings. One central leader stands out as the person of wisdom, the lecturer, and the authority figure. There is often a prescribed and closely followed order of service, and fellowship is relegated to a brief time before the meeting begins and at the close. Even those claiming to be much more organic, allowing everyone to have a voice, often appear to be one person directing the flow and offering balance or guidance whenever they deem necessary.

Something I've been pondering for a while now. What was the apostles' doctrine? For three and a half years, Jesus spent time daily with these twelve men He called apostles. Did He teach them doctrine, or did He reveal to them the kingdom? In the upper room, what was His message? He washed their feet, explained why, and told them that they should do likewise. He prayed for them to become one as He and the Father were one. Then He told them to love one another as He had loved them. He called that a new commandment.

When Jesus ascended into heaven, He told them to make disciples of the nations, teaching them to observe everything He commanded them. Was this the doctrine of the apostles the early church was steadfast in continuing? Ten days after Jesus ascended, the church began on the day of Pentecost with the conversion of the 3,000 as recorded in Acts 2. Did the apostles have time to write up a list of doctrines for this new movement to continue steadfastly in, or was it something else? As I asked this question, my mind began to think about Jesus's new command. "Love one another as I have loved you. By this, all men will know you are My disciples." Is it possible this was the apostles' doctrine?

As they daily went from house-to-house fellowshipping, breaking bread, and praying, they continued steadfastly pursuing love for one another. Is that what motivated those who had houses and land to sell it and lay the money at the apostles' feet? Is that why they sought to have all things in common? Love took care of those in need. The biblical pattern seems to be much more than a meeting in a designated house at a specified time with an order of service. It appears that this was a community whose common interest was learning to love one another as Christ loved them.

If there is anything we have to do, perhaps it is this. "A new commandment I give you that you love each other as I have loved you."

As I contemplated this way of thinking, a few things have happened. First, I noticed how often each of the apostles spoke of this subject of loving one another. Many repeated the words of Christ precisely as He had said. Second, the entirety of the epistles has taken on the tone of this command to love. Instructions regarding conduct, relationships, gatherings, etc. are far from being what we have made them into: laws, commandments, and church practices. They appear to be instructions and clarity on how to manifest love in the given situation. Situations interpreted as church discipline seem to be much more about preserving the integrity of the community of love and the love feast.

In my diminishing pursuit to do something, there is a growing desire to learn the ways of love. The love I'm desiring is the love Christ spoke about, the "as He loved me" kind of love. Yes, I know that kind of love is something I have to learn.

Recently there's something else I wonder if I'm supposed to do. It has to do with making disciples of the nations. I'm not suggesting that it is each of our responsibilities to disciple nations. I wonder though if we have an opportunity to do our part with those in our sphere of influence. I once believed that making disciples was the work of the ordained minister and only happened within the institution's four walls. Considering the number of people sitting in the congregation compared to the number of ministers on the stage means relatively few people are doing the work of making disciples. Once I no longer pastored a church, was I free from the charge to disciple the nations? I had friends, neighbors, and coworkers with whom I spent time, some daily. What responsibility did I have toward them? Was it to just live as a Christian and hope that they saw the difference in me? Was I supposed to be looking for opportunities or even creating the opportunities to share the gospel with them? Was I supposed to make it my goal to get them saved so hopefully I could get them into my church and my pastor could disciple them? Or am I put in those relationships to disciple them into Christ?

For eighteen years, I worked in the customer service field. For several years, I had a private office that allowed me to talk openly with my clients. As we came to know each other, many of them shared various parts of their life. I quickly came to understand I wasn't there just to listen to their stories. Nor was I there to give them some quick, spiritual, pat answers and tell them I would pray for them. Many of them were facing real-life situations. In a religious church setting, I could quickly share a couple of scripture, perhaps a story, and a bit of advice. In this environment, those things were often the last thing they wanted to hear. How do I develop a relationship with them that allows me over time to share a word that gives hope and offers the reality that Jesus loves them and is genuinely concerned with what they are going through? With some, it took months. With a coworker, it took nearly seven years. What started as a stone wall toward anything having to do with Jesus ended up being the thing we talked about often, especially His love and plans for them. The interracial couple, the alcoholic, and the biker in my neighborhood need to hear about the love of Jesus. How is that done? There is no method other than observing, listening, and waiting for the opportunity to speak to the issues of life they're facing. We should be able to say the words we speak, and the things we do are the words and actions we heard and observed from the Father. When we share the love of Christ with others, we are discipling the nations.

I suspect I could come up with many different ways I'm comfortable in showing love. Loving others the way Christ loves me needs to be more than a human or self-motivated act. The love I'm seeking to live has to come from Jesus and flow through me to anyone Jesus wants to show love. So yes, I guess I do have to do something. I have to stop all my doing and allow Him to be in and through me.

4

Relationships Before Traditions

EVENTUALLY, I BEGAN TO SETTLE DOWN. I EVEN BEGAN TO BE comfortable with having more questions than answers. At that point, I did what I now consider to be a dangerous thing. Dangerous, that is, if you mean it. If you do, you'd better be prepared to have the Holy Spirit take you seriously. I said,

> Lord, I'm not smart enough to know if what I believe is actually from You. I give every teaching regardless of who taught it back to You, and I ask the Holy Spirit to teach me all over again. Let me learn from Your Spirit. If nothing I've believed comes back, that's OK. I won't hold onto anything that does not come through the Holy Spirit's instruction. If You choose not to answer any of my questions immediately, I'm OK with the silence, with the not knowing. It's enough to know You.

I had no idea what that prayer would mean to my relationship not only with the Lord but with fellow believers. In hindsight, I realize this journey with the Lord hasn't been a linear timeline of events. Events in my life that have brought me to this point happened in no particular order. Several years before starting the church the Lord told me to walk away from, I spent a brief time pastoring a small fellowship. I learned some life-altering lessons in that fellowship, although at the time, I didn't know how important they would be to my spiritual journey.

I have never been a full-time minister. I have always been bivocational. When I began attending the fellowship, I had already been ministering for more than twenty-five years. I had just purchased a hardware store a year or so before, and now I was facing the possibility that the store wasn't going to make it. One day my wife told me that she had gone for a massage. The lady masseuse was also a pastor and had recently started a local fellowship. She felt led to share with this woman about my business. She told my wife that she wanted to come to the store and pray over it. I thought it couldn't hurt, so I said, "OK, set it up." During business hours, this woman showed up and proceeded to walk up and down every aisle, praying out loud, in tongues, and binding every foul spirit that held back the flow of prosperity.

A couple of weeks later, my wife said that this pastor planned a dedication service for her new church. Celeste felt like the Lord wanted us to attend and asked me to pray about it. My wife grew up Catholic, and although our church was open to moving in the gifts of the Spirit, we avoided the more extreme excesses of Pentecostalism. I had grown up with those excesses and wanted nothing to do with it. This woman pastor was just about as Pentecostal as anyone I had seen.

After some time in prayer, I knew we were supposed to go. Upon entering the room, I was immediately overwhelmed with the feeling that I had made a mistake. Sitting in the room were a few people I had invited to leave my previous church for various reasons. I considered them all to be in error by allowing practices and habits to detour them from the holy life of a sold-out disciple.

That night, she had asked some of the people I had disfellowshipped to contribute to the meeting. I would never do that. I believed that people who were not living 100 percent sold out should not serve in the congregational meetings. Enforcing that mindset never produced the desired effect of seeing them change. More often, it caused people to cover up habits, temptations, and the choices they made. Very few were good enough at covering up so that they were qualified to serve in the church. You can only cover up for so long before someone discovers your humanity or—worse yet—there's a public transgression.

A couple of years later, this lady turned the fellowship over to me. Yes, after that initial visit, we ended up attending that fellowship regularly. Once again, I was in the role of pastor. And then it happened; I began to become aware of my heart's attitude toward people; I didn't like them. Not liking people isn't the best of qualifications for a pastor. It seems to get in the way of effectively pastoring. I suspect it began several years before. It probably started with one individual I took a dislike to and refused to deal with it. Over time it no longer was individuals but types. I don't like the kind of people who _____ (fill in the blank). Once graduating to the dislike of the first type, others soon followed. Somewhere along the line, I probably had all the major types and all their subgroups on my list. I jokingly say that the last type on my long list was people who list the types of people they don't like. Yes, I even made it on my list.

Jesus began to show me how unhappy I was living in my world of dislike. It began to break me, and I knew I needed help. I didn't exactly know how to ask for help, but scripture told me that we could confess our faults one to another and pray one for another for healing. For several weeks, I'd get up behind the pulpit and talk about my list. I'd say something like "I've come to realize I don't like people. I don't even like you people." Maybe not the best thing for a pastor to say to the congregation, but I wanted to feel again. An older gentleman would yell out, "That's OK, Pastor! We love you!" Then they'd all get up and come around me to pray that God would complete the work He was doing in me. One day Celeste said, "If you're going to tell the people you don't like them again, I'm not going." I didn't need to. The healing had begun. I was starting to see them with new eyes, even ones I had disfellowshipped years before. I was falling in love with this fellowship of believers who were open with their struggles. Now so many years later, some of those believers remain friends.

Through that fellowship, I learned perhaps one of the greatest lessons of my life. My relationship with them through the Spirit of God is so much more valuable than the structures, rules, and rituals of conducting meetings. When did church become more about traditions than relationships anyway?

As the Holy Spirit began teaching me, many doctrines started to fade in importance. Things I held onto as being firmly proven by scripture now seemed insignificant. The walls I had built around the tenets of my religious affiliation began to come down. I found myself enjoying spending time with people from different Christian backgrounds. I enjoyed worshiping with them in ways that were foreign to me but familiar to them. Somehow, and perhaps because of our relationship, I found the beauty in it as I experienced their form of worship. I was now able to ask questions regarding the things they have come to believe without having preconceived ideas regarding the validity of their beliefs and practices. I realized that we weren't all that different in many of our views. I also discovered that as I practiced listening, I came to a much fuller understanding. I heard various perspectives from other vantage points. In some instances, this fuller understanding challenged my firmly held beliefs. In other instances, it answered questions I didn't even know I had.

Have you ever thought about the disciples, including who they were and what following Jesus required? All too often, Christianity over spiritualizes the people and events depicted in the Bible. What kind of relationship did James and John have with each other or Andrew and Peter? Was there sibling rivalry between them, jealousy, or a competitive spirit in any of them? Were the fishermen families of Andrew and Peter in competition with Zebedee and his sons, James and John, or vice versa? Was Matthew the tax collector the other disciples paid their extorted taxes? What about Simon the Zealot? Did he bring his political views regarding the violent overthrow of Rome into conversations around the evening fire? These twelve, who spent time with each other and the Lord, were learning to set those differences aside.

Every one of them had their religious tradition, practices, and philosophies. Now a rabbi was asking them to follow Him. It would take some time before realizing that they were being invited into a relationship, not just to accept a new philosophical set of beliefs, practices, and traditions.

From time to time, I'd hear someone referencing what they felt was the essential part of a church, which is the fellowship that should be happening there. One way I heard it was to compare it to a popular sitcom of the eighties called *Cheers*. The scene was a bar, and the primary idea was this was a place where "everybody knows your name." One fellow, also a regular, was greeted as he walked through the door, with everyone calling out his name.

The invitation the disciples received is the same one we have. It is more than coming to a place where everyone knows your name. If that's the extent of it, we have that with our corporate meetings. For years that's all I understood. I need to be in the place where I fit. The place where I am known for who I truly am. Is that desire idealistic? I realize I read into scripture things that might not be there. That's part of the questioning process.

In John's gospel, the fourteenth chapter, Phillip says, "Lord, show us the Father and it is sufficient for us." Jesus answered him, "Have I been with you so long and yet you have not known Me, Philip?" I have often thought about how sad those words are. Is it possible to spend three years with someone and not ever get to know them? In answer, I have to say I have set in buildings with people for years and never gotten past knowing their names and the names of their family members. We think we know someone if we know a few facts about them. We may not know them at all.

As I began writing this chapter, I thought about my experiences in congregational gatherings. I thought of two examples. I heard a story about a pastor of a good-sized church concerned with cliques within his congregation. For several weeks, his message was about being a family and the need to greet and fellowship with everyone, especially visitors. He spoke about going beyond our natural tendency to only gather with those of common interest. Seeing no change, he decided to do something about it. One week when there were a few visitors, while he was speaking, one of the deacons put up signs around the back of the room. Signs that said, "Fishermen gather here," "Quilters meet here," "Sports enthusiast over here," and "Visitors go ahead and greet one another. Chances are, no one from the congregation will welcome you."

Another congregation, one I knew personally, considered themselves to be a family. They spent a significant amount of time with each other outside of the meetings. Frequent times spent at each other's home, weekend barbeques, families getting together to take the kids to the park, even spending holidays with each other. They even printed a catalog of items individual members owned that they were willing to let others in the fellowship borrow. A few times annually, they had a workday to go to someone's house and do more significant projects. Projects like painting, garage cleaning, and building a toolshed. This same congregation knew how to celebrate each other. Birthdays, anniversaries, and other special days were made even more memorable in imaginative ways. When tragedy befell a member of the fellowship, and it did, they drew closer to each other.

My first assignment as a minister was as the overseer of a large communal house. The current overseer was moving to another position of ministry, so they needed to fill the vacancy. Driving a pickup I had borrowed with all my stuff, I began talking to the Lord. I assured Him that I would keep everything exactly as my predecessor had set up, including the daily work schedule for everyone who lived there. His practice was to require the residents to begin the day early with an hour of meditative prayer. What I heard in my spirit surprised me. "If I wanted you to do everything the same way, I would have left your predecessor in place. I'm calling you because of what you carry." I was only twenty-four, so I'm pretty sure I had no idea what I had to offer. I had to ask the Lord what that was. "Family, I want you to bring the concept of family to the residents."

I'm sure I didn't do everything right. I did try to consider how a sizeable family functioned. Instead of assigning tasks designed to keep everyone busy, I put up a list of the chores that needed to be done daily and asked everyone to sign up for the ones they were willing to do. In the beginning, I had to instruct on the willingness to all pitch in to get the necessary work done. I told everyone that as long as the chores got done on time, including meal preparation, I didn't care what they did with their free time. Free time was something many of them were unfamiliar with, at least in that setting. Christian communal houses and ranches were considered discipleship centers, which meant that you had to be busy doing something productive every minute.

No matter how many times I got called on the carpet for not exercising more authority, I could not bring myself to do anything that didn't look like family. When the communal days of the Jesus People Movement ended, many of us found ourselves struggling to build a local church. No longer living with each other, we were now beginning our careers, raising our families, and working with budgets. Our church life took on an entirely different feel from the relationships we had experienced while living communally.

I realized that many of the churches we built traded the closeness of family for structure and position. I began to desire an atmosphere that allowed everyone to have a seat and a voice at the table. Consider a large family around the dinner table. I realize what I envisioned might seem to be somewhat chaotic. I saw a sitting in which conversation took no particular order. Everyone was free to chime in with whatever they considered having value. It would be a dysfunctional family that would allow only the father, or perhaps the mature, to speak. Imagine requiring the remainder of the family to sit there night after night, dutifully hanging on every word. Could an open "dinner conversation" be considered a church service? Would it have value? How would a conversation of that manner compare to the weekly teaching?

I shared those thoughts with a few pastors, and more than once, the reply was "We tried that. It didn't work." I'd ask, "What do you mean you tried that?" We tried setting around tables and having a more interactive time during the message. People didn't like it. There it is. The traditions we've become accustomed to, and perhaps believe are most biblical, have to do with how we arrange the furniture while maintaining the basic structure of the meeting. We reserve relationship time before and after the meeting, not during. We encourage relationships to carry on outside of the congregational setting during the week.

Once I started thinking about everyone having a seat and a voice at the relationship table, I had to learn a few things. Love does not seek its own. The idea that everyone has a seat and a voice at the table starts with me. Do I honor the relationships I have? Does everyone have a seat at the table of my heart and life? Or am I content to attend a meeting where I only fellowship with a circle of those with common interests?

In a conversation, I need to give my full and undivided attention. In doing so, I'm saying this relationship has value. The honor of allowing others to fully express themselves in whatever manner or state they are in is perhaps one of the greatest gifts I can give. With that attitude expressed toward each other, more can happen in minutes than years attending meetings together.

One of the saddest things is that, in many cases, the world's philosophies and mindset have a more substantial influence on the church than the other way around. Over my lifetime, I have watched as we have become more distant from each other. Technology has a lot to do with this. Before many houses had phones and televisions, we looked forward to someone just dropping by to visit. A knock at the door caused a stir of excitement. Someone was coming over, and conversations would be enjoyed, with stories being shared—often with lots of laughter. Today it's considered rude to drop over to someone's house without first making an appointment. With some, there has to be a purpose for getting together.

At the writing of this book, we are in the middle of the COVID-19 pandemic. I have a friend in Texas who had been hosting occasional gatherings of believers from around the country. The purpose was to come together with each other in the presence of the Lord. No preset plan, no order of service, let the Lord be glorified in their midst and let Him direct their time. Worship and the sharing of the word would come from those gathered as the Spirit moved on individuals. Due to the pandemic, he was considering canceling these gatherings. As he sought the Lord for wisdom, he received a direction to go ahead in a way that honored the social distancing guidelines of the time. Rather than one large gathering, they would gather in several homes. Facilitating teams would rotate from home to home over the weekend. The testimonies that came as a result of listening to the Lord's plan were incredible. When we listen to the Lord for how He wants us to meet, God is honored. Honoring God always makes room for extraordinary things.

Over the past several years, there has been a growing dissatisfaction with the once-a-week meeting being the full expression of the Christian life. The result has been a mass exodus from the institutional church (IC.) New labels define those who have left but still maintain their relationship with the Lord: the "nones" and the "dones." As I have spent time away from the institutional church and don't like religious stereotypes, some consider me a none and a done. Nones means "none of the above religious affiliations." Dones means "done with the institutional meeting."

The idea that leaving a building designed to hold meetings and go to someone's home is somehow more biblical misses the point on so many levels. Our calling is to be members of one another. We are living stones joined together as a habitation for Him. It is not about the structure of how we get together that's important. It's the relationships of family coming together in the unity of the Spirit to represent Him to the world. Presenting Christ to the world will only be seen as we learn to love each other as Jesus loves us.

I have friends in probably every expression of worship style, including liturgical, orthodox, traditional, word-based, pentecostal, charismatic, and organic. As I consider the variety of personalities, I think that might have some bearing on meeting each person's style. Suppose you take someone out of the meeting environment that fits their personality and put them in another meeting format. In that case, they will usually gravitate back to what they consider a better fit. I've known people who grew tired of the structured church format and sought a more organic gathering. Shortly, they began to grow restless. The organic meeting style was excellent for a while, but they missed worshiping with a room full of people or missed someone with a deeper understanding of scriptures giving a sermon. The answer is not in attempting to come up with a one-style-fits-all format but to allow the variety of personalities within the body of Christ to find their rightful place within the family.

First Peter 2:5
You also, as living stones, are being built up a spiritual house, a holy priesthood, to offer up spiritual sacrifices acceptable to God through Jesus Christ.

Ephesians 2:22
In whom you also are being built together a dwelling place of God in the Spirit.

First Corinthians 12:26–27
And if one member suffers, all the members suffer with it; or if one member is honored, all the members rejoice with it. Now you are the body of Christ, and members individually.

Second Corinthians 5:16
Therefore from now on, we regard no one according to the flesh. Even though we have known Christ according to the flesh, yet now we know Him no longer.

The body of Christ represents every type of personality. Rather than the continual argument as to which style of meeting is proper or more biblical, why not seek how to manifest the oneness of Christ's body? This idea of the oneness of the body of Christ is something whose time has come. We, as living stones, are being built together as a spiritual house. I grew up in a Pentecostal home. I'm very familiar with that interpretation of the gifts of the Spirit. As a result, when I preach prophecy, even when I lead out in prayer, there is a recognized Pentecostal flavor. If I insist that my style is the only proper expression, it becomes divisive.

I wouldn't do that with, let's say, clothing styles. On most days, I'm most comfortable in jeans and a plain, colored T-shirt. I have a friend who, even on cold days, wears shorts, flip-flops, and a T-shirt with a message or a cartoon movie character on the front. It would be ridiculous if I tried to convert him to jeans and a plain T-shirt. What if

I refused to fellowship with him because he didn't dress the same way I did? I've heard it said that 10 a.m. on Sunday is the most divisive hour of the week. It doesn't have to be. It really could be just one or two hours of the entire week when people are free to worship Jesus the way they are most comfortable. For the remainder of the week, the body of Christ has the opportunity to manifest what it is to love each other as Christ loved us.

To do that, we have to come to the place where we no longer consider others after the flesh (i.e., how they dress or choose to worship). With whom is Christ putting you together? Are you attempting to get to know them after the Spirit? Are you learning to fellowship with them in the Spirit of truth? To do so, you have to press past personality styles. You have to learn to hear their heart, esteeming them as more significant than yourself.

As for me, my message to the body of Christ will continue to be family. Manifesting the family of God is so much more than just a phrase we use. I will always encourage others to learn the ways of a fully functioning, everyone participating family. I honestly believe this can and should happen with every group. I also think there is a way to incorporate family into every gathering. This unity of Spirit will not come about without some effort. Very few friendships happen effortlessly. I believe we can honor our traditions as well as the style of worship that fits our personality. The challenge is to allow relationships to take precedence over those traditions.

5

Dying of Thirst

I was looking down on a small group of people standing in a circle in my vision. They were standing around a small pond of rancid water. Each one was holding a water bottle. I noticed that each one was emaciated, was pale, had a drawn face, and was hesitant but preparing to fill his or her container and drink.

Suddenly I heard the voice of one as he began to pray, "Lord, thank You for this water in our desert. We're trusting You, Lord, that the rivers of revival You promised so many years ago are still coming. Give us patience, Lord, to wait for Your promise. Even if we die here in the desert, Lord, let us have confidence that a generation after us will live in that river." There was a chorus of amen as each began to draw water. What was so painful for me to observe was that I could see that they were standing on the bank of a rushing river from my vantage point. All they needed to do was get their eyes off their preconceived perceptions and turn around to see the river of God was already here.

How do you interpret such a vision? A few days later, without any real answers, I thought about the river of God. We live in a time when many in the charismatic circles I'm most familiar with often refer to being in the river. What is this river? I suspect most people would be referring to the river described in Ezekiel 47, so let's take a look and see if there is an insight into the vision.

Ezekiel 47 (NASB)

Then he brought me back to the door of the house; and behold, water was flowing from under the threshold of the house toward the east, for the house faced east. And the water was flowing down from under, from the right side of the house, from south of the altar. He brought me out by way of the north gate and led me around on the outside to the outer gate by way of the gate that faces east. And behold, water was trickling from the south side. When the man went out toward the east with a line in his hand, he measured a thousand cubits, and he led me through the water, water reaching the ankles. Again, he measured a thousand and led me through the water, water reaching the knees. Again, he measured a thousand and led me through the water, water reaching the loins. Again he measured a thousand; and it was a river that I could not ford, for the water had risen, enough water to swim in, a river that could not be forded. He said to me, "Son of man, have you seen this?" Then he brought me back to the bank of the river. Now when I had returned, behold, on the bank of the river there were very many trees on the one side and on the other.

Then he said to me, "These waters go out toward the eastern region and go down into the Arabah; then they go toward the sea, being made to flow into the sea, and the waters of the sea become fresh. It will come about that every living creature which swarms in every place where the river goes, will live. And there will be very many fish, for these waters go there and the others become fresh; so, everything will live where the river goes. And it will come about that fishermen will stand beside it; from Engedi to Eneglaim there will be a place for the spreading of nets. Their fish will be according to their kinds, like the fish of the Great Sea, very many. But its swamps and marshes will not become fresh; they

will be left for salt. By the river on its bank, on one side
and on the other, will grow all kinds of trees for food.
Their leaves will not wither, and their fruit will not fail.
They will bear every month because their water flows
from the sanctuary, and their fruit will be for food and
their leaves for healing."

As I studied this scripture, I highlighted a few things I saw. I've
heard sermons spiritualizing the various depths of the river. Something
I don't think I've ever seen before is that immediately following the
measuring of the uncrossable water, the man brought the prophet back
to the bank of the river. It was on the bank of the river that the prophet
saw many trees on both sides. After sharing a bit more about the river,
the man began talking about two things he saw on the bank. First, he
said, "Its swamps and marshes will not become fresh; they will be left
for salt." Then he began talking about the trees. He said they would
bear fruit year-round and the fruit would be for food and the leaves for
healing. As I pondered this portion of the prophet's vision, I began to
see an absolute correlation to the image.

Was this pond of brackish water one of the swamps or marshes of
the river? When reading Ezekiel's vision, I was intrigued by the phrase
"its swamps and marshes." Did the swamps and marshes belong to
the river? Were they part of the river at one time or another? Did they
get cut off over time from the flow? How did that relate to what I was
seeing, a group gathered around a swamp or marsh, considering that to
be God's provision?

The river brings healing to everything it touches. In one translation,
it says the river is teeming with life. It flows eastward toward Arabah,
which means a desolate or dry place, so how is it that something that
once was part of the river can no longer receive healing? What is it
that proceeds from the tabernacle that brings healing to everything it
touches? So many questions.

The more I asked, the more my mind began to jump from one
concept to another. I thought about the provision of the Lord for the
slaves in the desert after they left Egypt. They named it mana which

simply meant, what is it? They were only allowed to gather enough for the day. If they picked more than one day's portion the following day, they found what they had collected had rotted. Outside was fresh mana ready to be gathered for that day's provision.

Is the river like that? Not only is it filled with life, but it also brings life to everything it touches. The trees along its banks produce fruit year-round for food. The leaves of the trees bring healing. Is it possible to be in the flow of the river one day and the next day be gathered around a marsh of saltwater, considering that to be God's provision? Yes!

The river is constantly flowing, twisting, turning, always cutting new paths as it flows toward the sea. When part of that flow gets cut off, water that once was teeming with life begins to turn brackish.

I've been aware for years that the dreams, visions, thoughts, and impressions I've had that are not merely my ideas are most often about the body of Christ and the invitation to something more than what we are experiencing. This vision must have a deeper meaning than a simple "Make sure you don't get cut off from the flow of the Spirit."

From time to time, the body of Christ experiences a fresh wind of the Spirit. We know this wind of the Spirit by several names, such as revival, outpouring, visitation, renewal, and move. In a move of God, the Holy Spirit opens the hearts of many believers to receive a clearer understanding of God's very nature in ways past generations did not see. Perhaps an occasional voice from a past generation spoke of the unveiling or illumination, but often they were branded as a heretic. In a fresh move of God, it is that very revealing and insight that gives a more profound understanding of God's nature, purpose, and heart. It is that fresh insight that seems to give life to the movement. In Charismatic circles, the river of God is the expression of joy and freedom from that revelation.

I began my life in God in the Jesus People Movement. Freedom in the Spirit brought an incredible depth of joy. In hindsight, I now believe that the liberty and joy we experienced were by-products of being in the river; it was not the river. I watched several believers walk away from their commitment to faith when the excitement of being part of a movement ended.

New expressions of worship often accompany a fresh outpouring of the Spirit. Over time, those fresh expressions are turned into a style and promoted as the only acceptable worship. People begin going after the experience they have through this new expression of worship. I have come to believe that the river of God is God Himself. The river is the relationship we have with God. The further we press into that relationship, the deeper the river gets. When we allow ourselves, for whatever reason, to get cut off from that continual flow of relationship with God, the water we are drinking from becomes a swamp or marsh. Seeking an experience through a style of worship, rather than connecting with God, is drinking the bitter water. It won't satisfy your thirst.

The downside of the God and me syndrome I wrote about earlier manifests in several ways. Not just "I hear from God, and I don't need anyone telling me what He's saying." It also manifests as a resistance to becoming an integrated and functioning part of the body of Christ. A tradition that has cut many off from the river of a growing relationship with God is isolation. The most common isolation method is limiting our involvement in the body to corporate gatherings with the group of our choice. The apostle Paul gives insight into how God sees the church He is building and its intended effect.

> Ephesians 3:8–11
> To me, who am less than the least of all the saints, this grace was given, that I should preach among the Gentiles the unsearchable riches of Christ, and to make all see what is the fellowship of the mystery, which from the beginning of the ages has been hidden in God who created all things through Jesus Christ; to the intent that now the manifold wisdom of God might be made known by the church to the principalities and powers in the heavenly places, according to the eternal purpose which He accomplished in Christ Jesus our Lord.

Ephesians 3:14–21

For this reason I bow my knees to the Father of our Lord Jesus Christ, from whom the whole family in heaven and earth is named, that He would grant you, according to the riches of His glory, to be strengthened with might through His Spirit in the inner man, that Christ may dwell in your hearts through faith; that you, being rooted and grounded in love, may be able to comprehend with all the saints what is the width and length and depth and height—to know the love of Christ which passes knowledge; that you may be filled with all the fullness of God. Now to Him who is able to do exceedingly abundantly above all that we ask or think, according to the power that works in us, to Him be glory in the church by Christ Jesus to all generations, forever and ever. Amen.

Judging in any form cuts us off from a growing relationship with God. We do this when we consider that what we are learning from God places us on a higher spiritual plain than all other believers. Looking down on a new move contributed to the Holy Spirit is almost always done by those who were part of the Holy Spirit's last outpouring. They say this can't be God because it isn't coming the same way it did in our generation. It's also easy to consider any new revelation as being in error because it's different from what you understand. A listening ear and a hearing heart bring fresh insights and keep us in the river of relationship with God.

Some time ago, I spoke at a conference on the unity of the body. One of the other speakers shared on the ecclesia that Jesus said He would build. He presented an understanding that I had never heard before. Unity to me meant we would all come to the place where we saw things the same way. Attempts in the past to produce the oneness of the body of Christ were with other evangelical churches. If we could get the leaders of all the like-minded churches to have a few joint meetings annually, we could boast of having produced unity in our region.

This brother shared this type of unity had nothing to do with what Jesus said He would build, this thing He called ecclesia. The original meaning of the word is "assembly". Changing the word to "church" has come to mean any local congregation or the building. The word did not originate with Jesus. It was a word understood by the disciples to whom Jesus was speaking. It referred to any assembly of people and often implied a gathering for the specific purpose of establishing or forming some law or practice. There needed to be representatives from various philosophies and even political views within the community to be a true ecclesia. The multiple groups represented were called factions. The one calling the ecclesia together gave each faction a voice in the final decision process. In other words, an ecclesia was a sort of democratic town meeting to establish the structures by which they would govern.

Jesus declared to His disciples that He would build (call together) His ecclesia, and the gates of Hades would not prevail against it. This gathering of called-out ones would be coming from every philosophical faction. To each honor is given. I had never heard it presented this way before. It wasn't what I thought unity was. As I listened, I began to see in my mind a beautiful harmony. Somehow, I was able to see as the brother was speaking the possibility for this level of unity.

An illustration my father used with a group of men many years ago addressed the spirit of unity. He first shared from scripture, "In the multitude of counsel, there is safety and wisdom." He had everyone sit in a circle and then placed a cup covered with various pictures and graphics. He then said to each man, without moving your head from side to side, "Describe what you see." As he went around the circle of men, each shared something different according to what they saw. No man in that circle saw the entire picture of the cup. As each person shared, the image of the cup became clear. Not only does this demonstrate what a multitude of counsel is, but it is also an illustration of the Lord's ecclesia.

Flowing into the river is the many streams that make glad the heart of God. In the relationship with God through His ecclesia, healing comes to everything it touches. There is life in and around swamps and marshes but not the life of the river. The river is teaming with life.

God intends to display His manifold wisdom to principalities through the church.

> Ephesians 3:8–10
> To me, who am less than the least of all the saints, this grace was given, that I should preach among the Gentiles the unsearchable riches of Christ, and to make all see what is the fellowship of the mystery, which from the beginning of the ages has been hidden in God who created all things through Jesus Christ; to the intent that now the manifold wisdom of God might be made known by the church to the principalities and powers in the heavenly places.

> Ephesians 3:14–21
> For this reason I bow my knees to the Father of our Lord Jesus Christ, from whom the whole family in heaven and earth is named, that He would grant you, according to the riches of His glory, to be strengthened with might through His Spirit in the inner man, that Christ may dwell in your hearts through faith; that you, being rooted and grounded in love, may be able to comprehend with all the saints what is the width and length and depth and height to know the love of Christ which passes knowledge; that you may be filled with all the fullness of God. Now to Him who is able to do exceedingly abundantly above all that we ask or think, according to the power that works in us, to Him be glory in the church by Christ Jesus to all generations, forever and ever. Amen.

Far from being wrong, those who see things differently from how I see things may just be viewing from another vantage point, describing the part of the cup they're seeing. If I'm willing, if I listen intently, I can have a clearer understanding. Listening has come to mean that I hear more than just the words; I hear the backstory, what I call the *why*. Why do they view things the way they do? What experiences have they lived through that led them to their conclusions and their beliefs? If I truly desire to flow in the river of God, I have to come into the unity of the Spirit and the bond of peace. I may not now and perhaps will never see the part of the cup they're seeing; it's enough for me to hear them describe what they are seeing.

How people determine what they like in worship styles, and even meeting structures are often the result of personality differences. While I suspect these could become a swamp or marsh, it doesn't have to be. If one can keep their heart from a judgment of others, keep their heart free from my way is the right way, and keep their heart from trying to control others' form of worship and fellowship, they just might be drawing from the river of life.

After having the vision of people dying of thirst on the riverbank, I began sharing it with others. To my surprise, many I shared it with responded in similar ways. They said they were dying because they lived on the bank rather than living in the river. Because these were people I trusted, I started thinking maybe that is the complete interpretation. I started thinking of all the people I knew who seemed to have more zeal or passion for the things of God at one time or another. Now they seemed to be just living life, and God was relegated to one or two meetings weekly. I started a ministry called Riverbank Dwellers. I wanted to help those who left the excitement of living in the river to dwell on its banks. It appears that God is telling me that those who left the river were eventually going to die if they remained on the bank. I couldn't have been more wrong in my interpretation. I still hold on to Riverbank Dwellers' name, but the vision and purpose are considerably different from what I initially saw.

I tried to get my head around the idea of living in the river, but somehow, I couldn't see it. I live in a beautiful part of Northern California known as Six Rivers country. Over my lifetime, I've spent a considerable amount of time at each of these rivers. I've swum, fished, rafted, and boated in them. I've never lived in any of them. I'm not sure how one would go about doing that. I don't even see the prophet being encouraged to do that. Four times he was taken to the river and told to step in. Each time the depth of the water was more than the time before. After the fourth time, the angel brought him back to the bank of the river.

The first thing he saw upon returning to the bank was many trees on one side and the other.

> Psalm 1:1–3
> How blessed is the man who does not walk in the counsel of the wicked, nor stand in the path of sinners, nor sit in the seat of scoffers! ²But his delight is in the law of the Lord, and in His law, he meditates day and night. ³He will be like a tree firmly planted by streams of water, which yields it fruit in its season and its leaf does not wither; and in whatever he does, he prospers.

The angel told the prophet that these trees on the banks would bring forth fruit every month for food. The leaves would not wither and would be for the healing of the nations. The psalmist says the man who delights in the law of the Lord is like a tree planted on the bank of the river, yielding his fruit in season.

There is so much here that speaks to me. First, as I've already said, the river which is teaming with life doesn't appear to be something the Lord instructs us to live in. Drink from, yes. We can wade in it and even swim in it. You can even fish it, if that's your thing. Everything the river touches comes to life. I can't get away from the fact that the angel brought the prophet back to the bank of the river. What is it about the bank of the river? How does the vision I saw fit into the picture we see in Ezekiel's river?

We've already looked at the concept of the swamps and marshes on the bank of the river. Let's take a closer look at what life there is on the banks: the trees. Is this another picture of our calling, if you will, to be a fruit-bearing tree that provides nourishing food and healing? That would not be inconsistent with several pictural passages of scripture. He is the vine; we are the branches. Both fruit and leaves are part of the branches, not the vine. By their fruit, you will know them. A bad tree cannot produce good fruit.

One time, I was in a small town in the central valley of California. The main street of downtown was lined with orange trees laden with ripe fruit. It was hot, and I was hungry. Looking around, I didn't see anyone, so I reached up and picked one. I heard someone say, "That's why they're there." Just then, I noticed a business owner standing in the doorway of his shop. Embarrassed, I apologized. He said, "That's what they're there for. Pick a couple more for your journey if you want." As we talked, he told me that the city had planted them several years before for people to enjoy. The only thing they discouraged is someone picking more than they could enjoy in one day. That way, there'd be plenty for others.

I envision the trees on the banks of the river being every kind of fruit tree. Perhaps even a bit like the Garden of Eden must have been. If this is a picture of what the righteous are, fruit trees planted on the riverbank, we are a wide variety of every kind of fruit tree, not just a singular fruit orchard. To me, this is a beautiful picture of the body of Christ. Why do we get so hung up on insisting that if I am a pomegranate tree, I only want to hang out or be planted next to other pomegranates? We're not told much about these trees, just that they're fruit-bearing trees with leaves that have healing properties. In a previous chapter, I wrote about discipling the nations. I addressed the idea that each of us has specific spheres of influence: work, neighbors, family, or friends. We have the opportunity to provide those relationships with the fruit of our life that can give nourishment. What do you suspect it might mean that the leaves of the tree you are have healing properties?

Are you like those orange trees? That's what you're here for. Am I? One swamp that cannot sustain the life the Lord intends for us is the swamp of "It's all about me." Jesus saved me to give me a better life. I'm pressing in to get everything the kingdom has for me. My question is "Why?" And a follow-up is "How?" Is the reason you're pressing in so that the fruit of your life provides nourishment to those with whom you come into contact? Far too many I've met use some of the proper terminologies, but they are really in it for themselves, a better life, a reputation, the Father's blessing, etc. The sad thing is the deception of this mindset. It holds a person captive to a works mentality or legalism. Do whatever you consider is required to get from God the full benefits of a follower of Christ. It isn't about being a follower of Jesus; it's about the benefits. I realize this is a hard word. The question I'd ask is "What is the fruit of living that way? Are you refreshed, firmly planted, giving life to all who pass by and being a source of healing, or do you secretly have time in which you question if it's all worth it?"

Matthew 11:28–30
Come to Me, all who labor and heavy-laden, and I will give you rest. Take My yoke upon you and learn from Me, for I am gentle and lowly in heart, and you will find rest for your souls. For My yoke is easy, and My burden is light.

Hebrews 4:9–11
There remains therefore a rest for the people of God. For he who has entered His rest has himself also ceased from his works as God did from His Let us therefore be diligent to enter that rest, lest anyone fall according to the same example of disobedience.

Is that what Jesus meant when he said the greatest in the kingdom is the one who is servant to all? Does all the effort we put in working for the kingdom prove we are servants? Or did Jesus mean something entirely different by that statement? I'm amazed at how often people interpret Jesus teaching to be servants as applying only in church. Any consideration toward those in the world is in the form of evangelistic efforts or programs.

I somehow can't see that as being the heart of the Father or Jesus. A basic understanding of the life of Christ lets us know it wasn't. One of the hardest lessons I learned was that my calling in Jesus wasn't only for church. I became pretty good at performing for fellow Christians.

I knew how to act, how to talk, and how to socialize. I knew how to do everything necessary to be accepted in the Christian community.

I fooled myself into believing that the reason I wasn't as good in settings outside the church was that it was the world. You know if they hate you, it's because they hated Jesus. I found that I preferred living by what I considered to be the teaching and instructions of the epistles. The teachings of Christ were more complex. He was all about justice, mercy, and heart issues over the hard and fast laws of religious activity and performance. Am I really supposed to do good to those who persecute me? Or pray for those that despitefully use me? What about loving my enemies? Who does that? I don't even do that for people who go to my own church. If they don't like me, fine. I won't have anything to do with them.

I'm thinking about being a tree planted by the river with roots that draw in the water of life, causing the fruit of my life to nourish all who pass by stretches me. The challenge is to allow the Lord to change my heart's attitude toward people in the world. Maybe that line that determines how I treat someone is arbitrary. If I am in their life, even if only for a brief moment, can they taste the fruit of the way I treat them and see that the Lord is good? I think about how I've felt about the divisions I've set up. Drinking from the water of separation doesn't taste good. No matter how I try to flavor it, it doesn't refresh me. The excuses I've used—you know them: "the world hates Christians", "the world's getting darker and darker", etc. So I'll say "I love them (with the love of the Lord)", whatever that means, but not have much to do with them. I'll say "I'll pray for them", but I'll say a generic prayer that someone will reach out to them with the gospel. Maybe the world is getting worse and there is more hatred shown toward Christians because we're drinking bitter water, and our fruit reflects it.

6

First Works: First Love

IN MY FORTIES, I WAS SERVING AS AN ASSOCIATE PASTOR OF A CHURCH. On one particular Sunday, we had a guest speaker. I found myself thoroughly enjoying his message. He spoke about his observations regarding people he had known in his fifty-plus years of ministry. One of the comments was that; "Many of those who began their Christian life as teenagers or in their early twenties with such excitement and determination found themselves in their forties and fifties burned out, bitter, critical, frustrated, or disillusioned." His conclusion as to why this happened so often was that; "they simply gave up on their dreams." Today I find myself questioning that conclusion. While it is true, they lost sight of their vision. I doubt whether they *simply* gave them up.

The late sixties and early seventies saw an incredible outpouring of God's love on a generation of young people who knew they wanted to make a difference in the world around them. The desire to effect change caused them to challenge political, social, educational, and environmental systems. The sixties generation was a generation of young people who resisted the traditional values of racial segregation, women's subservient roles, and many other philosophies resulting from fear and ignorance. They demanded change. It was upon this generation that God revealed His love. Through this generation, which was labeled by many as being rebellious, God chose to bring change to the traditional religious system. It was these young people who dared to dream a dream of a church that *embraced* differences and called them the many-faceted expressions of Christ's body. They desired to see unity and not conformity, knowing the importance of each member contributing their part, building itself up in love.

They believed their generation could reach the entire world with the gospel. They knew they were pilgrims on this earth. They were ambassadors of a kingdom. So they went to cities, villages, countries, hamlets, and islands. Wherever there were people, they desired to bring the good news of Christ's love.

Today, the question is "Where is that generation?" While it is true that many are still serving God in a variety of ways, many are not. It is to those who are no longer pursuing their God-given dreams that I write. It doesn't matter what you are doing today. You might be in full-time ministry, part of a ministry support team, a congregation or home fellowship member, or no longer attending any formal gathering. Maybe you've given up on any religious experience.

Ask yourself this question: "Did I *simply* give up my dream, or did I systematically replace it with other pursuits?" Perhaps as you ask this question, you might discover you never knew what *your* dream was.

Whatever truths we hold in our hearts become the realities upon which we base our life. It is out of that reality that we live. In the sixties, we as a generation declared that we no longer wanted to believe our taught values. We said that all we need is love. Our observation was that materialism and capitalism became an open door for the greedy and the corrupt. It was indeed survival of the fittest (richest), and we didn't need any of it. A backpack and a bed roll were all we needed. We looked for community and enjoyed sharing everything. We believed each person was free to do their own thing and called it beautiful when they did. We expanded our minds as well as our philosophies. We traveled wherever the wind blew. Revolutionary thought became *"the cause."*

It wasn't long after the hippie movement began that the gospel of Jesus's love reached this generation, and the "Jesus People" revolution began. Whole communes were turning to Christ; witnessing teams went everywhere and saw daily conversions. Public beaches, street corners, city parks—wherever there was a Frisbee-throwing young person, those Jesus People were passing out their tracks with people bowing their heads and turning to Christ. Christian communes began to spring up everywhere, and the message of discipleship became the only message of importance.

We learned that the ideals we tried to live by were, in fact, true, that all the world needed was love. However, love is not a philosophy; it is a person: *God*. Simplicity is God's way. Examples of Jesus telling the rich, young ruler to sell all he had and give to the poor and how the converts in the book of Acts had all things in common excited our minimalistic ideals. Even our desire to travel and see the world was a good thing. In light of the scriptures that teach, we have no permanent dwelling place but are pilgrims and strangers in this world. As citizens of a heavenly kingdom, we are Christ's ambassadors to this world. Our generation would avoid all the previous generations' mistakes and would not lose sight of the goal.

There was a belief that was common among many of that generation. Anything having to do with the establishment was fundamentally wrong and must be changed or overthrown. It was that belief that caused much of the revolution of the sixties. This very belief is based on a judgment and is itself sown in rebellion. This core belief caused many not to trust anyone from past generations. Because of this, what could have been an opportunity to receive wisdom from older believers was often rejected. The result was a trial-and-error approach, making many unavoidable mistakes that caused some to walk away from the joy of their salvation.

The apostle Paul wrote to the saints in Galatia that they had started in grace only to end up in works quickly. Many of the Jesus People followed the same path. What began as a response to the love of Christ became a movement to start more Christian churches throughout the world. Personal discipleship gave way to pursuing the vision. Discovering your God-given gifts, your anointings, and your passions was replaced by striving for a position within the organization. When it was no longer popular to live a shared lifestyle, communes and discipleship centers shut their doors.

The exit out of a shared lifestyle became the beginning of a long journey to find some sense of normalcy. In some instances, this was an escape from the teaching they felt manipulated them to sell out to a bigger-than-life vision. For them, the movement and all associated with it were now just part of their history. The seeds of discouragement and disillusionment were planted in their hearts. They found themselves confused and searching for someone or something that could help make sense of it all.

Many others found themselves disillusioned, frustrated, bitter, or critical. Questions that have come up in many conversations I've had over the past several years are "Where did we go wrong?" and "What was that all about?"

Perhaps at this point, it would be healthy to ask a couple of questions.

- Do you understand that discipleship is a work of the Holy Spirit? It is a process that changes you from the inside out, conforming you to the image of Christ. While it often involves human interaction, it is not a method to be used by a group to conform you to their methodology or doctrinal interpretations.
- Do you understand that taking the gospel to the ends of the earth begins with the call to be a light and testimony to those with whom you are in daily contact?
- Do you understand that each of us has unique gifts, anointings, and passions? Have you taken the time to discover what those are?
- Have you taken time to discover where you fit in the overall plan of God?
- Have you taken the time to discover where you fit in His church?
- Have you replaced your gifting, anointing, and passion for seeking a position or office within a local assembly?
- Have you allowed a relationship based entirely on love and acceptance to become a pursuit of works and performance?

Today a message is reaching every generation. For the Jesus People generation, it isn't new. It's one we've heard before. For those of that generation, it is the very foundation of our Christian life. Even though the teaching is not new, it is coming with a new understanding. God loves you right now, right where you are. He accepts you today with all your hang-ups and failures. He has never been angry with you or frustrated because of your failures. He came to set us free, and for many of us, the things that had formed the biggest bondage were religion, legalism, and performance. We are hearing a message of God's grace, and it is setting us free. It is not unlike when we first received Jesus as our Savior. We were tired of our life. We were sick of the mess we had made, and we wanted to start over.

Today Jesus is saying to us, "Come unto me all you who labor and are heavy-laden, and I will give you rest for your souls. Take *my* yoke upon you and *learn of me,* for my yoke is easy, and my burden is light." The message of grace has been called the message of individual responsibility. You are invited to come back to the place where you first began, into a relationship—not with a church or a philosophy but with a loving God. We are being called again to discipleship, not man's idea of discipleship but the Holy Spirit's. The Lord is not asking us to submit to men but to come into a relationship of trust with a loving God.

I've talked with many who served the church as elders, leaders, overseers, fivefold ministers, shepherds, mentors, and spiritual fathers and mothers. Many of those same people are saying, "Been there. Done that. Worn the T-shirt." God is calling us all to return to our first love, to experience Him. He is calling us out of bondage into the freedom that belongs to the sons and daughters of God.

Let me encourage you to give your heart over to the Holy Spirit and allow Him to reveal the Father's love. Allow the Holy Spirit to quiet the voices of religion, performance, and legalism. Ask Him to replace those messages with the truth. Ask for the assurance of your worth in God. His message to you is that He accepts you right now. You are righteous because of Christ's obedience on the cross. Let Him remove the feelings of failure and insignificance. Allow the Holy Spirit to give you back your sense of destiny and fill your heart with your God-given dream.

Matthew 11:28–30 (MSG)
Are you tired? Worn out? Burned out on religion? Come to me. Get away with me and you'll recover your life. I'll show you how to take a real rest. Walk with me and work with me—watch how I do it. Learn the unforced

rhythms of grace. I won't lay anything heavy or ill-fitting on you. Keep company with me and you'll learn to live freely and lightly.

The older generation is once again experiencing an outpouring of God's love. We again hear the call to be "Jesus People," the called-out ones. A generation that began strong will be a generation that will finish strong, not in our strength but in our weakness, which becomes the place where He can be strong in us. Rest in His grace, embrace His love, know His acceptance, and let His Spirit breathe on you once again.

Younger generations are hearing the same call in a more divided world than it has ever been. Jesus invites you to learn of Him. His is the way of love that is so vast it changes everything it touches. The message is not overthrowing, but it's a message of transformation. The call is not to create more isolation but more spiritual inclusion.

A pastor friend of mine shared a two-part vision he had some years back. The first was a tsunami coming toward the West Coast of California. He said it came in just under the Golden Gate Bridge. The second was of a second, much larger wave washing over the Golden Gate Bridge. The interpretation he believed was that this represented two waves of the Jesus People Movement hitting the West Coast. If this is a true vision, I think we're about to see the second wave of the Jesus People Movement reach this present generation.

Jesus said He would build His church, and the gates of Hades would not prevail against it. This church Jesus spoke about was born in the first century and began on the day of Pentecost. Three thousand people were converted to the Jesus way. The church Jesus introduced was about a way of believing that transformed their way of living. It is the way of love. Love invites everyone to partake of Christ's offer of life. The message is simple. Jesus is the way, the truth, and the life. Jesus is the Messiah they had been seeking for centuries. Jesus as Messiah would restore them to a right relationship with God. The message is the same today; this is the gospel.

Those who responded to the message became part of the family. Teaching, which came in the form of the apostles' doctrine, was what the disciples had seen and heard from the master Jesus. It was the way of love. Everything the original disciples taught was about that love. It was the way they loved that would let all men know they were Jesus's disciples. The community of believers grew because of the invitation to receive God's love, which the believers demonstrated.

Jesus is looking for a generation that will respond in the same way. The simplicity of believing that those who have responded to the gospel by believing in Christ are now family. The instructions of Christ are the instruction of love. Build a community of believers who love one another and are openly sharing that love. All works have to be the result of love.

> First Corinthians 13:3
> And though I bestow all my goods to feed the poor, and
> though I give my body to be burned, but have not love,
> it profits me nothing.

"Receive God's love" is the call to every generation. Learning to live in and practice the way of love is our privilege.

7

What Is Love?

In the early eighties, while flying to Boston, the Lord told me that He was about to bring a new focus to the church. A pastor friend of mine invited me to hold a series of meetings in his church. I heard that familiar voice asking an unusual question. "Do you know the *one thing* my children don't know?" "Only one thing?" I asked. It seems to me that there are many things we don't know. He continued, "My children don't know that I love them." I answered, "Lord, of course, we know You love us. It's one of the first things we learn in Sunday school. Jesus loves me, this I know, for the Bible tells me so." Then the Lord showed me how often, when praying or prophesying over someone about how loved or accepted they were, they would break and begin to weep. Hearing words of love and acceptance would touch a deep place in their heart. He was about to reveal His love in a fresh new way. With that, the conversation ended.

So just how much do we know about the love of God, and more particularly His love for us individually? I dare say the majority of Christians give little thought to this subject of love. Many would conclude that God's love for the individual is more of a universal kind of love; in other words, God loves everyone, so of course, He loves me. Is that the extent of God's love for me? Over the years, the few times I considered the reality of God's love, I found myself once again with more questions than answers. Does God's love extend to the individual? Is that way of thinking selfish? Is God's love only global, as in "for God so loves the world"? Is God's love also corporate, as in first He loved Israel, and now He loves the church?

To each of the questions, the answer is yes. God's love does extend to the individual. I once had a vision in which I was standing next to a table. The top of the table was a beautifully painted picture. I don't know how I knew this, but somehow, I knew this was the painting of my own life. All of a sudden, I was lifted above the table. The higher I went, the more tables came into view, and the more pictures I saw. I knew these tables, each with a beautifully painted picture, were the lives of those around me. I became aware that the tables were interconnected. Each link revealed another picture. High above the original table, hundreds of tables interlinked into a panoramic view magnificent and beautiful beyond words.

When I focus on the picture that is God's love expressed in my life, I find the beauty of the image God chooses to display. As beautiful as that might be, it is not complete. When I expand my vision, I become aware of the larger picture created in the unity of those connections. Enlarging my field of vision, focusing on God's love for His church and ultimately for the entire world, allows me to see the beauty of the whole. It also allows me to see the beauty of each part that makes up the whole. I cannot separate the individual from the whole, nor can I separate the completed picture from the individual.

> First Corinthians 13:4–8
> Love suffers long and is kind; love does not envy; love does not parade itself, is not puffed up; does not behave rudely, does not seek its own, is not provoked, thinks no evil; does not rejoice in iniquity, but rejoices in the truth; bears all things, believes all things, hopes all things, endures all things. [8]Love never fails.

Now let's put these attributes of love together with how I view God's interaction with my own life. Scripture tells us that God is love. Therefore, it would not be a stretch to insert the word *God* in the place of the word *love* in this chapter. In other words, God suffers long and kind, etc. Either way, I think it is fair to say we may be missing something in understanding the reality of the statement "God loves me."

Did I switch things up? I started this chapter with the conversation I was having with the Lord about knowing that Jesus loves us, and now I'm talking about God the Father loving us. I've met many people inside and outside the church who say, "I know Jesus loves me, but to be honest with you, I'm not sure what I believe about God the Father." Then they follow it up with something like "I sure hope He loves me. I'd hate to get on the wrong side of God." Are Jesus and God able to be separated? Is that what Jesus taught?

One of the times Jesus displayed displeasure was when dealing with the religious leaders who were not accurately representing God. He rebuked them for creating a system that added more laws, ordinances, and statutes to those given by Moses. Jesus rebuked them for taking the seat of honor and expecting to be treated as superior to other Israelites and turning the house of God from a place of prayer for the nations into a den of thieves.

Jesus befriends the ordinary everyday person and the sinner. He makes a point of recognizing them, going to their home for lunch, hanging out, just one of the "good ole boys." On the other hand, God is the one who brings calamity and destruction to cities and nations because of iniquity. He kills people who hold back from giving Him everything (time, treasure, and talent): Ananias and Sapphira. "I will have vengeance on whom I will have vengeance." It's a fearful thing to fall into the hands of the living God, all the while believing that Jesus is God or, more to the point, that Jesus and God are one.

The heart is only able to hold one position on any given issue. It is out of the belief of the heart that we live. It is the belief of our heart that determines the reality of our perspective and worldview. Suppose our heart believes that Jesus and God act independently of each other. In that case, Jesus is forgiving, kind, full of mercy, and always good. God, however, is the Judge of the universe, ready to punish every transgression. The result is the way we live our lives will be in fear, not love. We'll somehow justify holding on to a distorted belief that God wanted to punish us, but Jesus stepped in to take all of God's wrath. I've met many Christians who believe when they sin, God wants to punish them severely. They consider themselves to sin quite often, but Jesus as an advocate reminds God that He died for them, that He loves them, and therefore God should show them mercy.

When your heart understands that Jesus and God are truly one, inseparable, our worldview, our view of God, and our perspective change dramatically. The core belief of your heart determines how you view God and is the basis of how you live. It is also that core belief that filters what you focus on when reading the Bible. If you hold in your heart the idea that God is the eternal punisher wanting to punish you every time you sin, you will only see the scriptures that seem to support that belief. Scriptures that talk about the mercy of the Lord, being dead to sin, or of love covering a multitude of sins are not seen, excused away, or ignored.

It's like the complaint I've heard on multiple occasions. Every time I drive downtown, every traffic light is red. Apparently, this isn't only true about our town, as I read a study in which they tested that statement. They concluded that the lights were red approximately 50 percent of the time, and 50 percent of the time, they were green. What does that say? If your heart focuses on red lights, you will conclude that every time the lights are red. This conclusion is not valid, but your mind doesn't register the times they are green.

With that in mind, let's go back to 1 Corinthians 13 and see how it fits when we replace the word *love* with *God*. God suffers long and kind. God is longsuffering, not willing that any would perish. God takes no delight in the death of the wicked. It's the loving-kindness of the Lord that leads to repentance. God is not jealous. Immediately, if you have even a basic knowledge of scripture, an argument comes up in your mind. Doesn't the Bible say God is a jealous God? I'm glad you're paying attention. To say love or God is not jealous has to be tied in with the following two statements: God does not brag and is not arrogant.

I know some people who hate when a promotion or blessing comes their way. They believe that if they accept any praise or recognition, a jealous God will punish them for attempting to share His glory. They live in fear that it's only a matter of time before the great equalizer comes to visit. Is God so arrogant as to have to send calamity to keep people humble? Pride goes before destruction and a haughty spirit before a fall. In the list of the things the Lord hates and are abominations, a *proud look* is the first thing listed. Is that only for humankind, but God is exempt? God resists the proud but gives grace to the humble. Perhaps we have misjudged God. He might be a little more like Jesus is.

I want to skip over the following two statements: "love does not act unbecomingly and does not seek its own." I believe we have already sufficiently addressed these points. God is not provoked, does not consider a wrong suffered, does not rejoice in unrighteousness, but rejoices with the truth and bears all things. We blame God for every disaster that comes. Natural disasters are called "acts of God." To accuse God of being the source of calamity is to misunderstand Him.

When a catastrophic event happens in a city, there is no end to the voices that are quick to point out the sin of the city God is judging. So let's get this straight: "love is not provoked, does not keep account of a wrong suffered, does not rejoice in unrighteousness, but rejoices with the truth and bears all things." Does that only apply to us as humans and more particularly us as Christians? Is God exempt from having to display this very description of love? Is that what we're saying?

I can hear the arguments that are coming up as you're reading this. Those arguments try to find a scriptural balance that lets God off the hook—allowing Him to bring calamity, destruction, and judgment because He is sovereign. After all, He is holy and just, and His judgments are righteous altogether. Love/God bears all things, believes all things, hopes all things, endures all things, and above all, love/God never fails.

To bear all things is to provide a "shelter in the storm." In Song of Solomon, we read, regarding the king, "He brought me to the banqueting table, and his banner over me was love." Providing a banner over us is what love/God does. He covers us and bears us up in his love. God believes everything He ever spoke over us. He holds in the hope of His love that we will embrace everything He put into us when He fashioned us—every gift, talent, and ability. In His endurance, He continues to surround us with His presence, even when we refuse to accept His love. He does this not because that's what love/God does but because that's what love/God is.

As I began to understand that I had a wrong idea of God and that one reason Jesus came was to give me a clear picture of who God was, I started taking a much closer look at how He treated others. I shared in a previous chapter that there was a time I didn't like people. I thought I was at the end of my list. In reality, I was at the top of my list. It was my deep disdain for myself that caused me to dislike other people. So much of what I didn't like about others I saw in myself. Under an entirely wrong concept of God, I could not possibly like myself when He was disappointed in me. The things I perceived opened the door for His displeasure, and the various ways I believed He judged and disciplined me kept me from knowing His love. I felt God as the great punisher allowed me to get caught more often than not so He could keep me on the straight and narrow.

I had an entirely wrong concept of discipline. I didn't see it as a loving father shaping my life (the literal meaning of the word *chasten)* to be the reflection of His love. Instead, I thought that everything wrong that ever happened to me was God's way of punishing me for all the bad things I had done. This concept of God punishing me blinded me to areas in which I needed to change. Often what I consider to be ways that God was punishing me were the results of the law of sowing and reaping.

Consider the person who has a wrong concept of what is secular and what is spiritual. They go to work because they have to earn money to pay the bills. They don't want to be at work; they'd prefer to hang out with other believers discussing scriptures. Rather than performing at the top of their game at work, their mind is adrift thinking about how they'd rather be with their Christian friends. They rehearse over and over what they'd like to be discussing. Because their mind isn't in their work, it shows. The boss, tired of poor performance, fires them. Now one of two things is concluded. Either it's because the enemy is bringing spiritual warfare or an attack against them or they consider this to be the Lord punishing them. Either way, they don't see the error of not understanding that there is no separation between spiritual and secular. To the believer, everything is spiritual. Whatever your hands find to do, do that with your whole heart as unto the Lord. The Lord's discipline is not to inflict pain or punishment but for correction. It is my responsibility to ask what needs to be corrected.

Now I was being confronted with the genuine possibility that I didn't know God at all. I'm not talking about the religious concept of being saved; I was. I'm sure if I'd died anytime during that period of my life, I would have gone to heaven. But I didn't know God. I knew some being, way up in heaven, who was so holy I didn't deserve to stand in His presence.

I think if I were alive in Jesus's day, He would have stopped to have a conversation with me. I suspect that conversation would have been filled with joy and would have spoken to the most profound need of my heart. I believe that because every conversation recorded in the gospels modeled that. The woman at the well in Samaria ended with "Come see a man who told me everything about my life." She wasn't shamed or condemned; she was set free and wanted to share it. That's what love does. Love brings out the pain buried in the heart so that it can remove it. Today Jesus reaches out to me to reveal who the Father is.

I'm growing in that understanding. The Lord is the one who came into the garden looking for Adam. Adam was the one hiding. The Lord made clothes that would be comfortable and cover their shame and their nakedness. The way they covered their nakedness was to sew fig leaves together. Not very comfortable; fig leaves are actually pretty scratchy. The Lord is the one who told the prophet Hosea to marry a prostitute. When she proved herself unfaithful, He told him to go out and find her and take her back into his home as his wife.

The Lord tells the parable of the prodigal son. I have heard it referred to as the story of the faithful and loving father. Perhaps that would be a better title for the story. Like Adam and Eve, have I ever done the very thing God told me not to do? Did the Lord seek me and cover my shame? Today I'd have to say yes on multiple occasions, like the prophet Hosea or like the king as recorded in the Song of Songs. He brought me to His banqueting table, and His banner over me was love. When I squandered away all that the Father freely gave me, having returned broken, ashamed, willing just to be a servant, He threw His arms around me and celebrated me.

The sad thing is that as long as I hold in my heart a wrong belief about God, and in particular what it takes to get God to love me, I never quite see it. Even when things are going right, I'm waiting for something to change. I know it's only a matter of time before I'm going to slip up and God's going to get me. God's love is so much bigger than overlooking when I mess up. "God so loved the world that He gave His only begotten Son." Jesus did not come to condemn the world but to save it. Jesus came to take the sin issue off the table, and Jesus only did what He saw the Father do.

The message of God's love for the individual, as wonderful as that is, falls short of the entire message of God's love. It can become a small body of water cut off from the flow of the river. The idea of God loving me, saving me, and drawing me into a right relationship with Him, although true, needs to fit within God's purpose for the redemption of man. For God so loved the world. He puts the solitary in families. In other words, God's love is about family. Individuals make up families, and it is the individual expressions that make each family unique.

Jesus told His disciples that He was giving them a new commandment: "Love one another as I have loved you." He said that the only way the world would know they are His disciples was by the love they had for each other. He spoke of the depth of love that would surpass the camaraderie of a local band of believers who all thought alike. This love He was talking about was something that would cause the world to take notice. This love must be more than agreeing on some justice issues. The love Jesus commanded calls us as individuals into the family of His choosing and His making.

Paul gives us some insight into what this family would look like by using the analogy of the human body. One part cannot say that I don't need you because you don't function the same way. He says if we all performed the same way, some essential functions would not happen. Christ desires that we express His love for those who function differently, including those who view life differently, interpret scripture differently, and have different interests and values and even different personalities. Christ's love is more than the religious rhetorical response of I love them. I have to. I'm a Christian. I just don't have anything in common with them, I just don't agree with them, or my all-time favorite: I just don't like them.

Two months after Jesus died, His disciples gathered in an upper room. The book of Acts records the event that took place. We often immediately think about the outpouring of the Spirit or Peter's message or the 3,000 souls saved. I want to focus on something I have missed for years. Remember Jesus telling the twelve to make disciples out of all nations?

> Acts 2:5
> And there were dwelling in Jerusalem Jews, devout men, from every nation under heaven.

There were devout men Jews from *every nation under heaven* dwelling in Jerusalem.

> Acts 2:9–11
> Parthians and Medes and Elamites, those dwelling in Mesopotamia, Judea and Cappadocia, Pontus, and Asia, Phrygia and Pamphylia, Egypt and parts of Libya adjoining Cyrene, visitors from Rome both Jews and proselytes, Cretans and Arabs-we hear them speaking in our own tongues the wonderful works of God.

Just a few days before, Jesus told them to disciple all nations. Here they are right here in Jerusalem, this new movement, followers of Jesus, from every country under heaven, who only have a religious understanding of God and know nothing of Jesus. The disciples had one commandment: to love one another as Jesus had loved them. How were they to disciple them? John gives us a bit of insight when he says what we have seen and heard and handled we have declared to you. What did they teach? I believe they taught how to love. In one place, the Bible teaches that if we love those who also love us, what reward do we have? Even unbelievers do that.

When I think of different nationalities living in Jerusalem, I think of the eight years I lived in New York. You could cross the street and be in an entirely different ethnic neighborhood—each with its own culture, government, practices, and beliefs. Was ancient Jerusalem any different? Now 3,000 people were identifying as believing in Jesus with varying cultural differences. The disciples taught those new believers to love each other regardless of the differences and seek a unity of Spirit that comes from learning to love each other in the same way Jesus loved them.

In addition to the cultural differences, there were political and philosophical differences that existed in Jerusalem.

- Pharisees observed all Jewish rituals and studied both the Torah and oral law. They were considered moderates in that they attempted to adapt the old codes of the law to their urban conditions.
- Sadducees: aristocratic conservative priestly class holding to the strict ancient doctrines; refusing to accept any oral law or anything not written in the Torah.
- Essenes: regarded religious observances in the synagogue and temple as corrupt; they organized communities in the wilderness of Judea, lived a monastic lifestyle, and practiced justice toward humankind.
- Samaritans accepted the Pentateuch as the only inspired scriptures. They were looked down upon by Jews because they were part of the dispersion, the Northern tribes carried away into captivity.
- Zealots were Jewish nationalists, opposed to Rome, who believed theocracy should be the law of the land. They advocated the violent overthrow of Roman rule.
- Scribes: Well-versed in the law of Moses, they recorded everything for those unable to read or write. Highly educated, they became spiritual and temporal legal counselors.

- Publicans: Public workers/farmers whose responsibilities included managing and maintaining public lands for Rome, including collecting taxes.

God's plan for today is to join people of every nationality, tribe, tongue, and political and philosophical persuasion and teach them how to love the way He loved us. Through this degree of love, He is going to reach the entire world. Jesus introduced this call to love as a new commandment, and He called it His command. Almost without exception, when asking a Christian what Jesus commanded regarding love, the answer they give is the one He gave to the lawyer attempting to test Him. When asked which is the great commandment in the law, Jesus answered, "You shall love the Lord your God with all your heart, with all your soul, and with all your mind." This is the first and great commandment, and the second is like it, "You shall love your neighbor as yourself. On these two commandments hang all the law and the prophets."

Do you see the difference here? This is not Jesus's teaching on love. This is Jesus answering a lawyer's question as to what the greatest commandment of the law is. Jesus's teaching on love is to love one another as He has loved you. The two commands upon which all the law and prophets hang depend on the individual. "You shall love the Lord your God" and "You shall love your neighbor."

You can interpret the new command from Jesus in a couple of ways. Both apply. First, it is a continual flow, as you are being loved by Jesus, love one another. The second interpretation is. in the same way I have loved you love one another. Both variations take the emphasis off you and place it on Jesus. You are no longer attempting to generate love for God and love for your neighbor in your strength. As you respond to the love of God through Jesus, you in turn give love to others.

This is why I can no longer convince myself that by simply joining a local group of like-minded people I am following Christ's commandment to love. With all the groups worldwide doing that, the world is still waiting to see the love that Christ commanded. The kind of love that would cause the whole world to know we are His disciples.

8

Broken-Down Planes

In April 2012, I had a dream. I knew it was from the Lord and knew it was about me. I was walking down a road. A cheaply made airplane landed on the street in front of me. The pilot, a man with unkempt hair and unshaven, dressed in old jeans and a faded flannel shirt, invited me to get in. Although he appeared to be around my age, it was apparent he had had a rough life. The plane was functional but in dire need of cosmetic repair. I got in, and we took off. Shortly after takeoff, he introduced himself. I recognized the last name as owners of several businesses in our community. He told me he worked for his family but wasn't one of the owners because he didn't measure up to his parents' and siblings' expectations. I said, "You probably don't know this, but I know their secretary; perhaps if I had known ahead of time, I could have called her and gotten a ride on their private jet." I then suggested we fly over to my place, and I would help him fix up this plane. As soon as I said that, he landed the plane and told me to get out. He then flew away and left me there. I started walking back toward the road. To get to the street, I had to climb over a fence and walk through what I thought was a big field. When I got into the field, I realized it was a graveyard. Then the dream ended.

To be honest, I don't really like this dream. It's too real and personal. It also has broader implications than just a personal interpretation. The invitation to enter the vehicle of another's life is a sacred honor. I didn't see it that way. I only noticed the areas that needed repair. Old, faded clothes and unkempt hair made it appear that life had not been easy.

Have you ever said something and even before it's out of your mouth you wished you could take it back? Scripture tells us it's out of the abundance of the heart that the mouth speaks. Those things that seem to come out of our mouths before we engage the filtering system are the words that reveal the deep thoughts of the heart.

Where is my empathy? Do I even really want to be on his plane? He invited me so it must be the right thing. Why then can't I see past the external and hear the cry of his heart? He's opening his life to me. What's the proper response? Whatever it is, my reaction was terrible.

There's a poem my dad quoted often. "The Touch of the Master's Hand" by Myra Brooks Welch speaks of the auctioning of an old violin for just a couple of dollars. Before the close of the bidding, an older man picked it up and played a beautiful melody. The price immediately went from a couple of dollars to a few thousand. The difference was the touch of the master's hand. The poem compares this old violin to the life of those discarded, pushed aside by the thoughtless crowd of humanity. A person's actual value is not seen in their accomplishments but in the melody of their life through the touch of the master's hand. We need to answer the question "Who is the master?" Although I would never have admitted it, I thought of myself as a sort of master for far too much of my life. It looked like this. I know Jesus is the real Master, but He has anointed me and given me the wisdom to know what others need to get their "out of tune" life in a place where He can play a beautiful melody.

I had a lot to learn, and even though I had been a pastor for almost thirty years, I didn't know much about shepherding the Lord's way. I remember all the training sessions I taught on leadership and shepherding. I focused on all the familiar scriptures regarding giving an account, watching for souls, feeding the flock, being overseers, etc. I was careful not to be accused of control by adding the warning to not lord it over God's people. In all of that instruction, I never saw the flaw. The heart belief that I was the master and everyone else, including whole congregations and even denominations, were old violins or, as I began this chapter, broken-down planes that needed me as the master to fix them. If I were the only one in leadership that felt that way, this would be a short chapter.

One day sitting in my easy chair, not thinking about anything, God spoke to my heart. "Get your Bible and go into your room. I want to talk to you about something." I thought, *That's weird, God has never spoken to me that way. Usually, He just breaks into my thoughts with His thoughts. He begins the conversation, and we start discussing and, on occasion, arguing. I argue. He restates. Sometime later, when I realize He isn't going to amend His statement based on the wisdom of my argument, I concede. This time, however, He is telling me to get my Bible and go to my room. OK, we'll try it this way.* Sitting on my bed with the Bible next to me, I wait. Hearing nothing, I decided to try something I had previously criticized: the "point and read method" of getting a word from God.

I flipped open my Bible and looked down; my eyes fell on this passage;

Ezekiel 34:17-23
'And as for you, O My flock, thus says the Lord God: "Behold, I shall judge between sheep and sheep, between rams and goats. Is it too little for you to have eaten up the good pasture, that you must tread down with your feet the residue of your pasture—and to have drunk of the clear waters, that you must foul the residue with your feet? And as for My flock, they eat what you have trampled with your feet, and they drink what you have fouled with your feet." 'Therefore thus says the Lord God to them: "Behold, I Myself will judge between the fat and the lean sheep. Because you have pushed with side and shoulder, butted all the weak ones with your horns, and scattered them abroad, therefore I will save My flock, and they shall no longer be a prey; and I will judge between sheep and sheep I will establish one shepherd over them, and he shall feed them.

By now, I was crying, but I was not exactly sure why. I was aware that I was reading something that had never stood out to me before. I was remarkably familiar with the idea of God judging between the sheep and the goats. But now I was reading about sheep and sheep.

Then I heard the Lord say, "I want you to do two things. I want you to identify with the lean sheep." Secondly, "I want you to find them and bring them to their Shepherd."

Now here's where the discussion begins. I said, "OK, but I have a question. What's a lean sheep?"

Immediately I heard this answer: "Someone who has made every attempt to be accepted by the fat sheep to no avail." Now I was weeping. I thought, *I don't have any problem identifying with lean sheep. I feel like I might be the leader of the pack.*

I had a lot of questions. How was I supposed to lead them to their shepherd? I was not a pastor any longer. I was not even involved with a fellowship. I also wondered how I would find them. What does it mean to bring them to their shepherd? I found out that many lean sheep no longer belonged to a fellowship, and some had given up the faith altogether.

It took me years to begin to understand the dream about the broken-down plane. I don't have to go out searching for lean sheep; they'll come to me. What I do have to do is listen to them, not just their words, their heart. I should have recognized the hearts cry in his statement. "I work for them, but I'm not one of the owners because I don't measure up to their expectations." Instead, I was only thinking, *I know that family. I have an in with them. I can get out of this uncomfortable situation by using my connections.* Looking back, I have to ask myself, "Do I want to identify with lean sheep?" How similar the story sounds to my own. Maybe it was my story. I was reminded of the thoughts I had when the Lord first spoke to me about the idea of there being lean sheep. *I don't have any problem identifying with lean sheep. I feel like I might be the leader of the pack.* How could I bring them to their shepherd as long as I saw myself in that way? Something had to change.

It was a year or so later when I was sharing this experience with a friend. He asked me if I read the first sixteen verses of Ezekiel 34. I told him, "No, I don't think so. At least not in a way that I could tell you what it says." He said, "Look it up. You might understand why there are so many lean sheep."

Ezekiel 34:1-16
And the word of the LORD came to me, saying, "Son of man, prophesy against the shepherds of Israel, prophesy and say to them, 'Thus says the Lord GOD to the shepherds: "Woe to the shepherds of Israel who feed themselves! Should not the shepherds feed the flocks? You eat the fat and clothe yourselves with the wool; you slaughter the fatlings, but you do not feed the flock. The weak you have not strengthened, nor have you healed those who were sick, nor bound up the broken, nor brought back what was driven away, nor sought what was lost; but with force and cruelty you have ruled them. So they were scattered because there was no shepherd; and they became food for all the beasts of the field when they were scattered. My sheep wandered through all the mountains, and on every high hill; yes, My flock was scattered over the whole face of the earth, and no one was seeking or searching for them."
'Therefore, you shepherds, hear the word of the LORD: "As I live," says the Lord GOD, "surely because My flock became a prey, and My flock became food for every beast of the field, because there was no shepherd, nor did My shepherds search for My flock, but the shepherds fed themselves and did not feed My flock"—therefore, O shepherds, hear the word of the LORD! Thus says the Lord GOD: "Behold, I am against the shepherds, and I will require My flock at their hand; I will cause them to cease feeding the sheep, and the shepherds shall feed themselves no more; for I will deliver My flock from their mouths, that they may no longer be food for them." 'For thus says the Lord GOD: "Indeed I

Myself will search for My sheep and seek them out. As a shepherd seeks out his flock on the day he is among his scattered sheep, so will I seek out My sheep and deliver them from all the places where they were scattered on a cloudy and dark day. And I will bring them out from the peoples and gather them from the countries, and will bring them to their own land; I will feed them on the mountains of Israel, in the valleys and in all the inhabited places of the country. I will feed them in good pasture, and their fold shall be on the high mountains of Israel. There they shall lie down in a good fold and feed in rich pasture on the mountains of Israel. I will feed My flock, and I will make them lie down," says the Lord God. "I will seek what was lost and bring back what was driven away, bind up the broken and strengthen what was sick; but I will destroy the fat and the strong, and feed them in judgment."

In this journey of relearning, I have made some very bold statements regarding the institutionalization of Christianity and church structure. As a result, I have been accused even by friends of being against the church. I am not against the church. I am learning to be more gracious with my words. I have a strong desire to experience what Jesus said He would build: a church against which that the gates of Hades could not prevail. As long as we are satisfied with the structures we have made, we will not press on for anything more.

When I read about the church Jesus is building, I see that He is the head. We all are the body. He has placed in His church equipping gifts: apostle, prophet, evangelist, pastor, and teacher. Besides, these equipping gifts are the gift of leadership. Those with the anointing to equip or to be in leadership do not own the sheep. They are there to serve the church. We are His people and the sheep of His pasture.

How does a leader lead someone to their shepherd? How do fivefold ministers equip others to do the work of ministry? These questions are some I've been asking the Lord for wisdom. So while I don't have a definite answer, the dream continues to speak to me.

I've been in many conversations on this subject. As long as our assumptions remain the same, we will come to the same conclusions. The word *leader* will always mean the one who sets the pace. *Setting the pace* means the leader sets the vision, gives instruction and direction, and makes all necessary adjustments and corrections. Far too often, scriptures like "Submit to your leaders" and "Obey those who have the rule over you" are used to justify a wrong concept of authority.

Sitting in a congregation are people who will never fit into any of the institutional leadership roles. They show up with uncombed hair, unshaven, faded jeans, and old flannel shirts. I'm not necessarily speaking literally. I'm speaking figuratively. In other words, they don't fit the mold of what we've set up as the image and qualifications of a leader. Outside the walls of the local assembly, it's a different story. Many of these same people are successful in various areas of life: businesspeople, entertainers, politicians, educators, dads, and moms.

How are Christian leaders equipping them to disciple the nations? How are Christian leaders serving and teaching them in hearing directly from the head of the church? So often, I have seen these people marginalized because of different pursuits. Church leaders determine that they're more interested in outside endeavors than in the local assembly's vision and following the direction of the leaders.

Jesus told His disciples that the civil rulers of His day lord it over those subject to them. He went on to say that among them, it would not be so.

> Matthew 20:26
> Yet it shall not be so among you; but whoever desires
> to become great among you, let him be your servant.

Those who desire to be great would be a servant to all. I think this is where we get the term *servant leader*. Is that what Jesus said: "You will be servant leaders"? I only know how to be a leader. Even with lean sheep, I saw myself as a leader. Would a servant care that the one he's serving isn't clean-shaven with hair neatly combed or neatly dressed? A servant leader might if his heart emphasizes a leader more than a servant. As long as I see myself as a leader, even if I call myself a servant leader, my attempts to serve are self-serving. First, masked behind the veil of service, there is a sense that I am in this person's life to fix them. Second, there is the sense that I know what they need to get their life together. Finally, should I be successful in helping them, there settles in my heart a sense of "job well done." Now on to the next person I can help.

The night Jesus was betrayed, leading up to His crucifixion, He washed the disciples' feet. Pointing to Himself, He told them that He was among them as one who serves. He called Himself their Lord and Master and then said, "if I do this for you, you must do this for each other." In this, Jesus was showing them the example of what authentic leadership was. True leadership is washing feet if that's what is needed. It's seeing the need of the moment and doing that for no other reason than meeting what's required.

Two more things I learned from the dream. Why did I think the plane needed repair because of cosmetic issues? The aircraft was the man's mode of transportation. The *what* that got him through life. What made me think that by going to my place, I could help him fix it? What made me think it needed fixing in the first place or that I was qualified to help him improve it? How often did I perceive others' planes to be broken down and in dire need of repair? Although I didn't want to, I had to admit that it applied to almost everyone I met. Was I drinking from another swamp or marsh? The idea that as a leader, I need to fix everyone else. I could point to a dozen scriptures that said I should. I have a duty, a responsibility to warn them, admonish them, exhort them, and even rebuke them "in love," of course. That's how a leader helps fix broken planes. Then how come it's beginning to taste like salty water? I'm not tasting the refreshing water of life.

One day, I shared with a friend that the Lord asked me to find the lean sheep in our county and shepherd them. In reply, he said I remember when you had that experience, and you said the Lord asked you to bring them to their shepherd. Now you're saying He told you to shepherd them. Misquoting what the Lord said wasn't just an innocent mistake; this went deep into the heart of what I believed. I am doing what the Lord asked me to do when I set myself up as the shepherd. Isn't that what Peter said to shepherd the flock of God?

> First Peter 5:1–4
> The elders who are among you I exhort, I who am a fellow elder and a witness of the sufferings of Christ, and also a partaker of the glory that will be revealed: Shepherd the flock of God which is among you, serving as overseers, not by compulsion but willingly, not for dishonest gain but eagerly; nor as being lords over those entrusted to you, but being examples to the flock; and when the Chief Shepherd appears, you will receive the crown of glory that does not fade away.

There it is; it couldn't be more precise. I was supposed to shepherd the people I was gathering. I would just be careful that I did it in a manner that didn't offend anyone. I'd be careful not to lord it over anyone. Within a few months of joining, a member of our fellowship came to me and said he would be moving on. I knew he had been hurt in past church relationships and was very suspicious of getting involved. He said; "You talk a good talk, but your actions don't back up your words." When I asked him what he meant, he said, "You gave me a position, then began micromanaging every detail." I left no room for him to exercise his gift or explore how the Lord might lead him to function. It was a huge misunderstanding and one that was easy to clear up, but with the backlog of pain he was carrying, he wasn't willing to give it a second chance. I learned a great deal in that conversation and wished I had the opportunity to make amends.

My training, both by instruction and example, has been that as an overseer, I have the responsibility to see that everything fits the goals and direction I set. I see an example in Moses that permits me to say, see to it you do it precisely as I told you.

In the conversation with my friend, who reminded me that the Lord said to bring them to their shepherd, he asked me a challenging question. "If God asked you to bring them to their shepherd, how are you doing that?" I wasn't comfortable with my answer. "Well, I'm trying my best to pastor them." I don't know why I can't get it right the first time I receive instruction from the Lord. It would sure make it easier if I did.

Since that conversation and the experience with the man who felt lorded over, I have sought to understand how someone can function as a shepherd of those they walk with while bringing them to their shepherd. It took a long time to see that the two are not in conflict with each other. To lead them to their shepherd is not to abdicate any responsibility for careful oversight. To shepherd God's sheep the right way is to teach them how to allow the Lord to be their shepherd. It is to teach them how to hear the voice of their shepherd for themselves and follow that voice. Hearing His voice starts with knowing who the shepherd is.

As I think about the dream, I had to acknowledge that I was walking; he had the plane. Wow! There is something to that. How did I miss it? It is beginning to come together. Jesus is not asking me to find lean sheep but to be myself. Those that need whatever the Lord has given me would stop and pick me up. We would have the opportunity to travel together. It may be that the means of travel would be a homemade plane in need of repair, but if it flew, that's good enough to get us to where we're going. At least that's what I think I'm supposed to get out of the dream. If the man were to ask me if I knew anything about planes, I could let him know if I did. Then it would be up to him to ask if I would like to help him work on his plane. Meanwhile, I'll enjoy the ride, and once we land, maybe I should get a bucket and a sponge and wash the aircraft.

So I didn't handle that too well. Now I have to get back to the road, to my journey. I have to climb this fence and walk through a field, and I'm back. What a waste of time. I tried to help him. He should have taken my offer. I mean, I could have arranged to fly in his family jet. Instead, I got in his broken-down plane. He's so ungrateful. Hey, what's this? I'm not in a field. I'm in a graveyard? I suspect the Lord wants me to know that I need to bury something, but what? Could it be my attitude? Why did I need to judge the man by outward appearances?

Why did I notice the areas that needed repair instead of the fact that he had built a functional airplane? Why did I have to establish that I knew someone who worked for his family? Worse yet that I could use my acquaintance to fly on something so much better than what he was offering.

Did that statement reveal an opinion I had of myself that I was deserving of so much more? Why didn't I hear his heart? I'm not sure I even listened to his words. I did hear the Lord say, "I want you to identify with the lean sheep." Lord, there is much that needs to die, wrong attitudes about my worth that now seems so self-righteous. I get it, Lord! Help me spend as long as I need in this graveyard burying all my wrong attitudes and the ways that do not bring healing.

> Psalm 23:1–6
> The Lord is my shepherd; I shall not want. He makes me to lie down in green pastures; He leads me beside the still waters. He restores my soul; He leads me in the paths of righteousness For His name's sake. Yea, though I walk through the valley of the shadow of death, I will fear no evil; For You are with me; Your rod and Your staff, they comfort me. You prepare a table before me in the presence of my enemies; You anoint my head with oil; My cup runs over. Surely goodness and mercy shall follow me All the days of my life; And I will dwell in the house of the Lord forever.

"The Lord is my shepherd; I shall not want" is a bold statement. For most believers, the list of needs is long. In speaking about lack, I'm not talking about the latest gadget or big-ticket item to improve your status. Scripture says that we need nothing because the Lord is our shepherd. There was a time I was teaching young leaders that if someone in your church is going outside the church to have their needs met, you are failing as a leader. That's an unbearable pressure under which to labor. I have a hard enough time with my immediate family trying to meet every need. If we aren't teaching people how to allow the Lord to be their shepherd, we are laboring under an impossible and human-made challenge.

Giving the Lord His rightful place as our shepherd is to allow the Holy Spirit to lead us. The Holy Spirit's influence on our hearts convinces us that we are children of God. As children of God, we are joint heirs with Jesus. Paul says, "If we suffer with Christ, we will be glorified with Him," and, "There is a glory to be revealed in us." The glory He had with the Father He gave us. God is the Father of glory. We are sons and daughters of God with a revealing of glory in us. How is that glory going to be revealed? We must come into the experiential knowledge of Christ in us, His unified body, is the hope of glory. Christ in His body is so much more than a nice sentiment or holding some form of mystical application. The revealing of God's glory will only be complete as the body of Christ lays aside the divisions of looking to certain leaders to be their shepherd and allows the Lord to shepherd His body. The Lord shepherding His body begins with the individuals who find their rightful place within His body.

9

As a Man Thinks

I FINALLY ANSWERED THE QUESTIONS ABOUT BEING INSANE TO MY satisfaction. I'm not, but I did conclude that I had many mixed-up ideas about what being a spiritual person means. I was coming to understand that it is so much more than the way we conducted ourselves in public, and especially at church. The long list of rules we grew up with that were supposed to prove our Christianity only succeeded in modifying our behavior. Underlying attitudes, in many instances, remained the same.

Remember what I said about functioning as a pastor yet not liking people? It's like a person who doesn't enjoy children becoming a teacher or a person who has no people skills becoming a customer service rep. It doesn't make sense. In an attempt to compensate for a negative attitude, we overcompensate by external performance. It wasn't just my story; it seemed like I met many people having a similar identity crisis. Church leaders teach about the promises of God, which God freely gave us, yet they struggle right along with the rest of us, trying to get them to work in their life. The struggle to get the confessions of our faith to work out in our life became why my fellow pastor and I wrote the *Foundation of the Heart* seminar. Christians make statements like "I believe every word written in the Bible." Yet when you look at their life, you see them struggling, trying to apply the very things they confess to believe. In the writing of the seminar, I began to understand that the primary reason is that we seldom allow the word to change our hearts. If we're honest, we may not even know how to let the word change us.

My understanding has always been that the primary emphasis of scripture is that we are supposed to do the word of God. After all, isn't that what James says? "Be doers of the word, and not hearers only." I had spent my entire adult life trying to do what I read in scripture. I taught others to find out what the Bible says and do it. In the time of my searching, I read what Paul wrote to the church at Colossae.

> Colossians 2:20–23
> Therefore, if you died with Christ from the basic principles of the world, why, as though living in the world, do you subject yourselves to regulations—Do not touch, do not taste, do not handle," which all concern things which perish with the using—according to the commandments and doctrines of men? These things indeed have an appearance of wisdom in self-imposed religion, false humility, and neglect of the body, but are of no value against the indulgence of the flesh.

Wow. That's a bold statement, and I'm sure some take it to the extreme. As I looked at this portion of scripture, especially in light of the belief that we had to do everything the Bible commands, questions flooded my mind. "These things have an appearance of wisdom and self-imposed religion". These things Paul says are "in accordance with the commandments and doctrines of men". This line of thinking led me to ask, "What was the apostles' doctrine spoken about in Acts?" As I began pondering that, I also started thinking about the counsel of apostles in Jerusalem discussing the work of Paul and Barnabas among the gentiles. The conclusion was that they didn't want to trouble the gentiles with a long list of rules.

Paul continues to say that this list of "self-imposed religion was of no value against the indulgence of the flesh". That statement challenged my way of thinking. Obeying the commandments found in the Bible was the only way to refrain from the excesses of the flesh, wasn't it? Paul is saying no, it's not. So how do I refrain from indulging in my base nature?

Before I go any further, I need to expand on why giving in to my fleshly desires was wrong. My early Christian teaching was that the flesh was evil. In my flesh dwells no good thing and if I sowed to the flesh, I would reap corruption. Ultimately that corruption would result in eternal punishment. Additionally, the understanding was that the flesh was carnal and was the fullness of my sinful nature. Now Paul is saying that keeping the rules was of no value against the indulgence of the flesh. If not, what are the means to overcome?

As long as I believe that I can overcome my flesh through religious observations and practices, I continue to have the cart in front of the horse. Jesus did not come to give us a new set of rules but to transform us into His image. This transformation requires a whole new way of thinking. This new way of thinking begins with changing the beliefs of our hearts.

I had always considered my flesh to mean my sinful nature. In other words, the lust of the flesh, the lust of the eye, and the pride of life. What is behind each of these things is the actual definition of the flesh. It is a belief buried deep within the heart of every person who says, "I am the center of my universe." This belief is individualized and manifests itself in uniquely personal ways.

> Romans 12:2
> And, do not be conformed to this world, but be transformed by the renewing of your mind, that you may prove what is that good and acceptable and perfect will of God.

Throughout our lifetime, we adopt beliefs that shape our personalities and in turn our actions. We read in Proverbs, "As a man thinks in his heart, he is." Our reality is the culmination of the core beliefs of our hearts. These heart beliefs are the result of events in our life to which we have given significance. Assigning significance to events in our life triggers our emotions. The stronger the emotion attached to the event, the stronger the need to answer why. It is this need to answer why that becomes the foundation of a core heart belief.

Why do things like this always happen to me? Why do people always treat me this way? Why does God allow these things in my life? These why questions, when answered, become the source of judgment about ourselves. The conclusions we make about ourselves become the foundational belief of our worth or value to society. In answering why, we form the basis of the judgments about humanity, including the classifications we create. Ultimately, we judge the existence of God and His involvement in the events that have happened in our life.

What I hold as my core heart belief shapes my personality and becomes my reality. Discovering those core heart beliefs is difficult as they lie beneath a myriad of supporting evidence.

Many of our heart beliefs are judgments we've made about ourselves, others, and God. Those we've formed about ourselves become the foundation upon which we live.

The glass-half-full person has formed a belief system that sees all of life in the best possible light. Challenges become opportunities for advancement. Trials are invitations to see how God is going to work things out. They seek to find a reason to be thankful for everything they are experiencing. Even in the darkest moments of life, they reach out to see the light. They live in the understanding that weeping only endures for the night; joy comes in the morning. Their reality is that their life is one blessing after another.

The glass-half-empty person has formed a belief system that even questions the events that seem favorable. Rewards, promotions, or complements solicit comments like they had to say that or it's about time. Their reality is life is hard. Any good that comes their way has to be earned. Both the fatalist and the victim are essentially glass-half-empty people. The fatalist believes that whatever is going to happen will and there is nothing that can stop it. The victim believes that they are on the receiving end of bad things from every source.

The beliefs of our hearts establish our reality. The thoughts of our hearts are the foundation of our worldview. It is the filter through which we draw our conclusions. Moral and political views are the expression of our reality.

Several years ago, a friend invited me to speak at a local Women's

Aglow meeting. While preparing, I had a mental picture of a very narrow road with a cliff on each side. One had the name Grace. The other had the name Discipleship. As I prayed about the meaning of the picture, I gained this understanding. Navigating the road of kingdom wisdom keeps us from falling off into an overemphasis of any one truth. I think the reason these two words came to me was that I had already fallen off the cliff of grace. I came out of a ministry that was strong on discipleship. My emotional response to that period caused me to embrace a new paradigm. My initial acceptance of the grace message was off-center.

Your reality causes you to give much more weight to any scripture that seems to support your view. Other scriptures that present an opposing view are not acknowledged, or you will reinterpret them to fit your idea. One person can only see scriptures that point out the severity of God. Scriptures that talk about the day of wrath seem to leap off the page, dismissing the myriad of scriptures speaking of mercy or grace. Another person only sees scriptural instruction regarding their role as a church leader. They require absolute submission because they are going to have to give an account. They demand recognition and even honor because scripture says that we need to know them who labor among us and are over us. If someone were to share about not lording over or being the servant of all, they would conclude that they're only doing what the scripture requires of them.

As a young minister, I joined in on so many conversations criticizing others' understandings and teachings. Anything that did not perfectly line up with my knowledge and interpretation of scripture was fair game. At some point, I realized I was only arguing with like-minded people against something I heard someone say about what someone else believed and taught. I hadn't read anything from the source, nor had I listened to any direct teachings. Quotes that are taken out of context to prove my argument don't count. It was then I began the practice of researching the matter. When I heard an emphasis or teaching that someone claimed was solidly biblical, I would go into research mode with an open mind and under the Holy Spirit's guidance. I can't tell you how many times people warned me. The warnings were usually about the danger of reading this or that author. Others would say to me how dangerous it was to listen to those despicable heresies. They reminded me of the grand deception from the antichrist's spirit to deceive even the elect. I found out that there are elements of truth in much of what I read. I'm frequently presented with positions and understandings that I've never heard before and therefore never considered. We get offtrack or go over the cliff when we go beyond the degree of truth revealed by the Holy Spirit. The most common way we do that is to conclude that this new insight is the fullness of revelation on the subject. If we have the complete revelation on the subject, then anyone who believes differently is wrong. Older generations tend to do that when those younger claim to have insights that differ from the familiar. Going beyond what has come through the inspiration of the Holy Spirit means that we supply answers to questions He has left unanswered. It's OK to share what we have Spirit-led revelation on and leave it at that.

The second type of reality is an agreed-upon way known as a collective or social reality. The statement of faith, or the "we believe" statements of a denomination or local church, are more than a document on paper. It is the glue that holds the group together. I realize many would argue with me on that point. Some would go so far as to say they don't even know what the church's statement of faith says. If practices, worship styles, or weekly sermons reflect a collective reality that goes against your reality, you will leave that group. When you find a group whose practices, worship style, and messages, for the most part, line up with your reality, you settle in. For most people, the limit of their Christian fellowship is with those who hold to the same.

In this area of collective reality, we see the most significant division between people and groups, each pointing to select scriptures to prove that their position is the most biblical. Emphasis like social justice, discipleship, grace, holiness, and restoration of the offices emphasizing apostolic authority are just a few of the Christian faith's personal and collective realities. Denominations that form around understandings that come in a move of God's Spirit are often more resistant to anyone with a different perspective.

There's a third reality called objective reality. Objective reality exists regardless of what you personally or collectively believe. In other words, objective reality is God's reality. God's reality is the complete revelation of God and His kingdom. Objective reality is more than the collection of information and its conclusions. To know God and the reality of His kingdom is to experience Him in His fullness. No one has a complete understanding of God's kingdom. For me, just knowing that God's reality can be accessed is the motivation behind continuing to ask questions.

As long as the body of Christ insists on staying divided over individual and collective realities, we will continue to miss the revelation of God's truth. How can I come into the fullness of experiencing all that God has for me? It may be an obvious statement, but I believe it begins with the understanding that I don't know everything. The things I think I know need to be subject to adjustments. That being the case, I need to open myself up to godly relationships, those relationships God puts in my life. Consider what is usually the standard practice in relationships. Two people form a friendship. In conversation, they come to a subject in which there is a stark difference in personal reality. Each person digs in and tries every way possible to convince the other that they are wrong. Depending on the strength of the relationship, it may end there. If they have a strong bond, they will probably agree to disagree and never bring up the subject again. Occasionally friends choose a third alternative to continue the battle of wits for the sport of it.

One of the messages that became a core value in the group I belonged to for twenty-five years was purpose and vision. The teaching was that the purpose of God is in all things, God would receive glory. The vision of God was threefold. These three aspects were to be given equal weight and pursued simultaneously: that each person would be conformed to the image of Christ, that we would proclaim the gospel to the whole world, and that the body of Christ would come into unity.

I tried everywhere I lived to bring about some level of unity between churches. Over the years, I've joined and started many different ministerial associations, all with little or no long-term effect. We formed some of those unity groups around a commonality of practice, worship, and doctrine. We would get together occasionally for a combined service.

More often than not, however, they just became coffee time with fellow pastors. Attempts to bring together a variety of denominations often failed over doctrinal issues. One was saying if you're going to let people who believe such and such come, I can't fellowship with that.

I spent a good deal of time asking God about that. How is the body ever going to become one? I still don't have an answer, but as long as we hold tight to our personal and collective realities, we won't get there. A few years ago, I invited various leaders to join me for a weekend getaway. On that weekend, I met Henry Hon. Henry is an author and lecturer on the subject of the ekklesia. Henry shared what he had come to understand regarding the word *ekklesia,* which most translations of the Bible translate as "church." Unfortunately, this is a bad translation. A better translation would be "assembly" or "gathering." The word predates the beginning of the church. The Greeks and the Romans used the word *ekklesia* to refer to a sociopolitical entity based upon citizenship in a city or state. *Ekklesia* is the word Jesus chose to use when He described what He would build. The book *One Ekklesia* by Henry brings out an interesting scripture.

> First Corinthians 11:18–19
> For first of all, when you come together as a church, I hear that there are divisions among you, and in part I believe it. For there must also be factions among you, that those who are approved may be recognized among you.

At a sociopolitical assembly, Henry shared that there needed to be factions. When I first heard this, I thought, *What is this guy saying?* As he continued, he noted what was referred to as factions were the varying positions held by the citizen of the community. Those who are approved are the leaders who can hear the various factions and make an informed decision. The approved know how to draw out the wisdom and understanding that came from the representations of the various factions. The challenge is how to allow for factions without becoming factious.

As long as I limit my fellowship to those of the same collective reality, I will be limited in the amount of objective reality I come to know. We have to be open to being fitted together with people of other viewpoints. Open dialogue is needed. Conversations that challenge our reality take time. They take a genuine desire to hear the other person. Not just the words that are coming out of their mouth. It requires hearing the backstory. What's behind their understanding? How did they come to see or interpret scripture in the way they do? Is there a way that their insight and your understanding might stretch each other and give you both a broader perspective? You will never know until you practice listening with an openness to learn. Some things are so strange that you may not be able to accept them at all. It's OK to hear someone else's reality without needing to fix them or embrace their beliefs.

It is essential if you want to see the ekklesia Jesus described to be willing to have our realities examined, challenged, and even adjusted. Earlier I referred to Romans 12:2. One of the Lord's methods to transform us is in hearing those who have a different understanding or interpretation of scriptures. Transformation comes as our teacher, the Holy Spirit, confirms in our heart the things that are of the kingdom. Remember not everything we have come to accept as either personal or collective reality touches on objective reality. One thing is true: growing in our understanding of God's reality requires being open to hearing other perspectives. As our hearts respond to a new and more profound knowledge of the kingdom, our reality is changed. In that transformation, unity happens with those who we previously may have considered wrong in their understanding.

10

Is This Church?

WELL, OVER THIRTY YEARS AGO, WHILE PASTORING IN NEW YORK, I had two very significant dreams. The first began as I drove into a parking lot. I was seeing before me three geodesic domes. The one on the right appeared to be the church. A long, tubular corridor connected it to the other two, which sat one in front of the other. I assumed these must house the Sunday school classrooms and probably the church offices. I entered the one I believed to be the church. What I entered was a gymnasium. My only reference point regarding churches led me to think they must have used this gym as a multipurpose facility setting up and tearing down when needed to conduct services. A few moments later, a man entered. As we began talking about the church, he said that the building was a gym for the community. The church gathers in dome number 2 down the hall. He also said that the church would be gathering in about a half hour.

As I entered the second dome, I saw what today I would recognize as a coffee shop. There were small tables with mismatched chairs filling the room. I looked for a stage but didn't see one. There was an area with a counter filled with an assortment of pastries and an espresso machine. Sitting at one of the tables was a woman reading. I asked if I could sit next to her, and we began talking. I asked her what kind of church this was. I had never seen anything but pews or chairs set in rows all facing the front. Here there was no front, and the chairs were not in rows. She chuckled and simply said, "Isn't the church wherever two or more gather in His name? The church will be gathering together in just a few minutes." Not understanding what she was getting at, I changed the subject and asked where the leaders sit. "Anywhere they want to," she replied.

Moments later, people began filling the chairs around the tables. I noticed most had small coolers or brown lunch bags with them. Some came to the counter and ordered coffee or a pastry. I heard a man begin to sing a familiar worship song, and no more than a few notes into the song, instruments joined in as well as the entire gathering. No sooner had that song ended than a woman's voice began another song, and again the instruments and group joined in worship. After the song, someone began to share an experience he had, followed by another sharing a portion of scripture that went along with the first person's experience. More songs, more sharing, then requests for prayer followed by groups of people gathering around the person who made the request, simultaneously lifting their voice in prayer. This open meeting continued for a couple of hours when a man's voice from somewhere in the room simply said, "It's been good to be church together. May the Lord bless our meal; let's share lunch." With that, people opened their coolers or brown bags. Some went back to the counter for more pastries or coffee. Still others went into the third dome, where there was a library of books, music, and teaching tapes; remember this dream was in the mid-eighties. Many of those in the dome enjoying lunch began sharing a portion of the meal they had brought with others. There seemed to be a real sense of family, hospitality, and generosity.

Between the two domes, I could see gatherings of people in a true spirit of fellowship. Some gathered around tables to enjoy their lunch, others had their Bibles open and were looking at a portion of scripture, small groups gathered for prayer, while others were deep in conversation.

When I woke the following day, I knew I had seen something of significance but honestly had no example to understand the dream. Our church was renting another facility at the time. It was always my desire to have our own building. Being from California, I thought, *If we were to build a church with three geodesic domes, that would be a drawing factor.* So I sketched out what I had seen, thinking, *Someday I'll take the sketches to an architect and maybe, just maybe, build the dome church.*

A couple of weeks later, I had a second dream. I pulled into the same parking lot. This time instead of the three domes, there was a long building. I was pretty sure this was the back of the Sunday school annex. I entered a side door to see a room filled with workers erecting walls. They were using construction tools of every sort, and sawdust covered the floor. One of the men told me that the sanctuary was completed and I should go check it out. Walking down the hall, I opened a side door into the sanctuary, and what I saw took my breath away. What served as a floor was grass. Yes, green grass. The entire ceiling was a series of skylights or perhaps a glass ceiling; I wasn't sure. The walls were a vibrant forest green with mahogany wood trim. On either side of the steps leading to the platform was the most beautiful array of live flowers. Behind the stage were a stone wall, a waterfall, and a pool. The front entry into this room entailed three sets of glass doors I estimated to be twelve to fifteen feet tall. Above the doors were windows that stretched out ten feet on either side and were perhaps eight feet tall. Over that series of windows, another set of windows was probably six feet tall, centered and matching the three pairs of doors' width. All of this trimmed with deep red mahogany to make the shape of a cross—a beautiful mahogany and glass cross.

As I stood admiring the architecture, people began to enter, carrying lawn chairs and coolers. They set their chairs up in random order, some facing the front but most in circles or just wherever they put them down. As the place began to fill up, a door to the side of the stage opened and a full orchestra and choir all dressed in tuxedos came out and took their place. Once in place, they began worshiping. As soon as worship began, most people got out of their chairs. Rather than stand and face the front, they began what looked to me like milling around. A few went and stood in front of the stage, joining in worship. I saw groups of people talking, some with open Bibles, some praying for one another. Those who remained seated seemed to be just talking. Sometimes people would come over and join in the conversation.

After what appeared to be a couple of hours, a man walked up to the center of the stage, picked up a microphone, and said, "As we conclude our gathering, I want to draw your attention to the entryway. Can you see it? We all came in through the cross. I pray blessings on your lunch and encourage you to enjoy the rest of our time together." People returning to their lawn chairs began enjoying the lunches they had brought. As in the first dream, many people shared what they had brought with others, making sure no one was left out.

Again, I missed the point. I thought about the beauty and the uniqueness of the structure. I thought it strange that the choir and orchestra were dressed in tuxedos while everyone else was in ordinary, everyday clothes sitting in lawn chairs. Other than being upset that the majority was not engaging in worship, I paid almost no attention to what was happening in those small circles. As with the first dream, I drew what I had seen, attempting to get the structures and colors right. Maybe this would be the church we would someday build.

As I think about these two dreams, I no longer focus on the buildings, as unique as they both were. I also don't know if I had ever seen or perhaps want to see a corporate gathering that functioned exactly like either of these two dreams. I think about how far we have come away from the simplicity of doing life together.

To attempt to give a literal interpretation to any part of these two dreams is to miss what I believe is the central theme. In both, I immediately determined which part of the building was for what specific church function. As to the domes, I mistakenly decided which one appeared the most like what I thought a church should look like turned out to be a public gym. What is it about our buildings that is so recognizable that even one dome right next to two others must be the church? In the second, I determined that I was entering the Sunday school annex.

The gentleman in the gym and the lady sitting at the table spoke of the church gathering together, not the people coming to church or church would be starting soon. I honestly had never heard it put that way before. I remember how comfortable they were sitting around the tables. I've occasionally set up the meeting room with tables and chairs, and the majority of those in attendance are anything but comfortable.

There are comments like "What's going on? Why aren't the chairs set up in rows? Are we going to have to talk?" The following week when the chairs are back in their rows, it's like a deep, settled peace enters the room.

The body of Christ cannot get away from coming together. Gathering together is not the issue; it's the value we place on one type of gathering over another. "Whenever two or more gather in My name, I am in their midst", which is the only prerequisite of being church together. If we cannot see that as being every bit as valuable as going to a public meeting, we miss the very essence of assembling as Christ's body. When our focus becomes more about the building's décor or the quality and the order of the service, we miss out on the intent of Christ's body coming together. The more who gather together in one locale, the stronger the pull is to organize it.

I've often thought how wonderful it would be if our times were as relaxed as an evening spent with friends just being together. Picture a large table where everyone not only has a seat at the table but a welcomed voice. Does that mean everyone will speak? Not necessarily, but maybe. Does it mean that some might monopolize or dominate trying to direct the conversation? Possibly, but probably not. Remember these are friends coming together to enjoy the fellowship of the evening in the presence of the Lord.

The scripture most often used to support our need to attend a weekly meeting is Hebrews 10:25. "Not forsaking assembling, as the habit of some, encourage one another, and all the more as you see the day drawing near." If one just reads or quotes that scripture without putting it in proper context, the conclusion is that the command of scripture is church attendance. Is it necessary to sing songs and have a formal sermon to feel like we've been to church?

> Hebrews 10:19-26
> Therefore, brethren, since we have confidence to enter
> the holy place by the blood of Jesus, by a new and living
> way which He inaugurated for us through the veil, that
> is, His flesh, and since we have a great priest over the

house of God, let us draw near with a sincere heart in full assurance of faith, having our hearts sprinkled clean from an evil conscience and our bodies washed with pure water.

Let us hold fast the confession of our hope without wavering, for He who promised is faithful; and let us consider how to stimulate one another to love and good deeds, not forsaking our own assembling together, as is the habit of some, but encouraging one another; and all the more as you see the day drawing near. For if we go on sinning willfully after receiving the knowledge of the truth, there no longer remains a sacrifice for sins.

The instruction of this scripture is that we would encourage one another to love and do good deeds. Encouraging is one of many "one another" scriptures. The idea of *one-anothering* is that we are engaged relationally with each other. The intention of our assembling is to be relational much more than formal.

I think of the scripture that says the whole body of Christ is built up by what every member supplies. In the way most services are conducted, is that a reality? In First Corinthians 14, Paul instructs us concerning public gatherings. In verse 26, he says that each one has a psalm, a teaching, a revelation, a tongue, or an interpretation. He then admonishes that everything is done for the purpose of edifying. Seeking to edify is part of learning to be a servant.

Regardless of the physical structure of the place we meet, our coming together needs to provide an atmosphere where every member is free to contribute. Contributing does not mean that everyone needs to share something every time. There are only so many who are comfortable speaking in a public setting. Even if you make the meeting so safe that anyone can speak up, some will never contribute in that way. Why is this? To make room for each member to do their part, we need to understand the body.

First Corinthians 12 Paul instructs us concerning the body. He compares it to the parts of the human anatomy. 'If the foot says I am not a hand; therefore, I am not part of the body, is it not for this reason any less a part of the body'? 'Or if the ear says, because I am not the eye, I am not part of the body, is it not part of the body'? Paul explains that 'if the whole body were an eye, where would the hearing be'?

In every locale, wherever a part of the body of Christ gathers, you will see eye people, ear people, feet people, and hand people. Depending on the size of the gathering, you will find a wide variety of giftings and callings. Each member is unique in their calling. It is through this uniqueness that God desires to build us wholly into Him. Through each unique expression and as we learn to contribute who we are within the body, the whole body becomes more like Jesus.

In the years since these two dreams, I've begun to ask more questions about what I saw. Did I see the whole vision? As much as I saw, I've been stretched to desire and believe for more than we presently experience. Now I find myself asking if the purpose of these dreams was to show me a more relaxed way of coming together regardless of numbers or format.

I have friends in almost every major Christian denomination. As you can probably imagine, their worship styles widely vary, as do their doctrinal beliefs. What day you must gather, with its pre-gathering preparations, and how you must conduct yourself while gathered together vary from group to group. These two dreams can't be about just another way to gather together. I honestly don't think so. While these dreams can be challenging to find ways to promote a more open gathering that allows everyone to have a voice, I believe there's still more.

I would accept that either of these two ways of coming together fits the narrative. How is it, brethren, that when you gather everyone has a song, an exhortation, a teaching, etc.? The larger the gathering, the more difficult it is to see the fulfillment of this gathering style. Depending on the structure of your group, either one of these could serve that purpose.

> First Corinthians 14:26
> How is it then, brethren? Whenever you come together,
> each of you has a psalm, has a teaching, has a tongue,
> has a revelation, has an interpretation. Let all things be
> done for edification.

Whenever doesn't mean when there're fewer than twenty. Nor does it mean at certain prescribed times in a prearranged location. Another "whenever scripture" is "Whenever two or more of you come together in My name, I am in your midst." We love to make commandments and formulas out of scripture. For many, an example might be that coming together in His name means we are intentional about getting together with other believers. Part of the intention for gathering is to accomplish a specific purpose; this becomes a rigid format.

During the years Celeste and I were not attending a local fellowship, people would often ask us where we were going to church. Most of these people would agree with the statement that a building is not the church. We are. Yet they were asking what building we go to and called that going to church. I would often answer something like "Well, let me see. This week for a while, I experienced church at Costco, at the service station while filling my gas tank, at the park, and right now here in the grocery store with you. Wherever I am with other believers, I am enjoying church." Some got it, but most just laughed it off and said something like "No, seriously, where are you going to church now?" I have friends who have written me off as backslidden, friends who pray for me, friends who don't get me, and friends who wish I'd get off the antichurch trip. I am more prochurch than I have ever been. For the first time, I'm beginning to understand who the church is.

In asking how Jesus is doing in building His church, I feel we must complete the statement. The gates of Hades cannot prevail against it. It started with twelve, then seventy, 120, and on the day of Pentecost, 3,000, and the number grew daily—ordinary people who chose to follow Him. In one generation, they turned the world upside down. From the shores of Galilee to the streets of Rome, the gospel spread, and the church grew.

Let's consider the possibility, a reality in several nations, that we did not have buildings in which to gather. Does that mean that the church does not exist in that locale? I hope we would all answer with a resounding no. In fact, in many places where it is illegal to gather in large assemblies, the church is growing. Steady growth is what the first-century church experienced. I can drive by several buildings that have housed portions of the church that sit empty and in dire need of repair in my hometown. While still conducting meetings, others have only a handful of attendees in a once-filled sanctuary.

There is a current move away from the institutional gathering. Millions have identified with the labels "nones and dones." "Nones" are those who, when asked regarding religious affiliation, would check the box "None of the above." "Dones" are those done with institutional gatherings.

My journey led me to listen to those identifying as a none, a done, or both. I have read books on the subject. I have sat with people and listened to their stories. I have also seen resistance from many believers to consider that something is happening in this transition with God's hand on it. Accusations such as rebellious, bitter, wounded, and even backslidden are the more common responses. What if God is at work? The problem with accusations is they're seldom correct and often based on preconceived judgments. Is it possible that this fits within the parameters of the teachings of Paul?

> Romans 14:4, 10, 13, and 19
> Who are you to judge another's servant? To his own master he stands or falls. Indeed, he will be made to stand, for God is able to make him stand. But why do you judge your brother? Or why do you show contempt for your brother? For we shall all stand before the judgment seat of Christ. Therefore let us not judge one another anymore, but rather resolve this, not to put a stumbling block or a cause to fall in our brother's way. Therefore let us pursue the things which make for peace and the things by which one may edify another.

As individuals, we need to allow God to join us with whoever He chooses and learn to be comfortable with His choice. If you enjoy a more corporate setting, that's fine. Many I know and fellowship with do. My encouragement is to ask God for wisdom to establish a more open relational time to gather with others. Start with two or three and resist the temptation to organize. Remember the primary focus is on allowing everyone to have a voice at the relational table.

If you have left the corporate gathering, do not isolate yourself. Ask God to show you who He has brought into your life. Seek to find a way to enjoy genuine fellowship with other believers. Above all, keep it real.

11

Individuals in Community

I WAS STANDING ON MY PORCH ONE MORNING, ENJOYING MY COFFEE. A question formed in my mind that I recognized as the beginning of a conversation with the Lord. "How do you view the church?" Not only is that a loaded question, but there are also various ways to answer. What came to mind was *How do you view the stream your church is part of compared to all other denominations, streams, or networks of independent churches?* As that question formed in my mind, I saw before me a set of stairs. On the lower steps written on the risers were the names of the many denominations. I don't remember the exact order, but they were Catholic, Lutheran, Methodist, Presbyterian, Baptist, Pentecostal, etc. On the top steps, the words written on the risers were *Latter Rain, Healing, Faith, Charismatic, Independent, Jesus People, Renewal, Apostolic,* etc. Then I heard, "Isn't this how you see the church, with your current understanding or denominational structure you ascribe to as the most important?" I had to admit that was precisely how I viewed my church. I had left the denomination I grew up in and embraced a more current move of God. The denomination of my childhood was several steps below my "top step."

Immediately in my mind, I saw myself hovering over a vast building. The roof was transparent, so I was able to see the rooms. What I saw were hundreds of rooms crowded with people. Again, I heard a question. "What's missing?" This time I was able to answer. "There are no doors, only walls. The people remain in whichever room they find themselves in." I then heard, "True, but what if there were no walls? The walls are unnecessary."

The walls we put up to safeguard our perceptions and beliefs have become our bondage. We call it by many names, traditions, foundations, apostolic doctrine, or progressive revelation. Regardless of what we call it, we believe ours is the only correct interpretation of scripture. Not realizing that the same walls have become a prison, keeping us from discovering the wisdom within the body. Additionally, we miss the understanding that our insights rest on the foundational truths of those who have gone before us. It is a continuum of God's revealed and living word. The revelation of God's word should never become a separation wall. Jesus Christ, the word of God, is the Way, the Truth, and the Life. Our understanding even of Him is in part. The "my reality is better than yours" syndrome puts up separating walls without a door. It's the spirit of competition.

Social media has become a tool that allows people to defend their preferred style of worship, the doctrines they consider most reflective of scripture, life choices, and social justice issues in a broad public forum. Perhaps because there is no face-to-face encounter, the defense is sometimes cruel. It is this tenacious defense that keeps us held captive behind walls without a door.

I discussed this very thing a few days ago with friends and made the following suggestion. Not one of us has come to a position we feel needs defending without a *why* behind that position. That *why* is often a journey of experiences, lessons learned, and a myriad of other things that shaped that perception, such as growing up in a home that held to a specific belief. The *why* might be a life event that jars you from your current perception to an entirely different view. Different positions have a definite reason for the conclusion; the backstory allows me to understand. When I take the time to let someone who holds a different perception share their story, I have an opportunity to allow Christ to open a door in our relationship. As I listen to their account or the *why* behind that conclusion, I understand their position better. While I may not embrace the same beliefs, I can appreciate how they arrived at those convictions. When I take this approach, three things happen. First, the other person no longer feels the need to defend their position viciously. Second, it opens the door for them to hear my story and conclusions. Understanding each other is the beginning of walls coming down, potentially leading to a harmonious and loving relationship. Finally, it allows both of us an opportunity to have our understanding adjusted.

If you desire to find a community or church that is doing everything right, the spirit of competition might be guiding your decision. Doing things right has a wide range of interpretations, not the least of which that it must conform to our particular taste in worship style, delivery of the message, and perhaps even social and economic makeup of the congregation, finally the doctrinal exegesis of scripture. The bottom line is we have already decided what is best. If it is genuinely best, it must be suitable for me.

The question to ask is "With whom is God putting you together?" Two thoughts from scripture might shed a bit of light on the assembling process of the church God is building. The first one is that He sets the members in the family as it pleases Him. The second is that He is fitting us together into a habitation for Himself. Allowing ourselves to be placed together with those of God's choosing is markedly different from finding a group that's doing everything right. Who has God already put in your life? Seek to know the why. Why am I connected to this person or these people? Am I getting to know them after the Spirit? Do I have a mutual giving and receiving relationship?

One principle of kingdom life is to become a giver. To the measure you give, you will receive. A downside of joining a community with everything already being done with excellence is that it leaves little room for you to add your flavor or become a true giver. Your contribution doesn't add to what is already perfect.

> Ephesians 4:16
> from whom the whole body, joined and knit together
> by what every joint supplies, according to the effective
> working by which every part does its share, causes
> growth of the body for the edifying of itself in love.

First Peter 2:5
you also, as living stones, are being built up a spiritual
house, a holy priesthood, to offer up spiritual sacrifices
acceptable to God through Jesus Christ.

The church God is building is held together by what everyone supplies. In the same way, it builds itself up in love. Each member is a living stone being fitted together into a holy habitation for the Lord. The Christian community needs each member to function as the individual God created with their giftings, talents, and abilities.

Before seeking a community to join, I'd suggest you spend time before the Lord asking tough questions. Do not settle for easy answers. Seek the mind of God in everything. Realize that the principles of the kingdom often go against what we would view as common sense. They also go against many of our religious teachings. His ways are not our ways. I pray that the Lord may lead you and show you His heart as you seek to find those with whom God is placing you in His dwelling place. The place where you can be who you are and where you can become an instrument that enriches the journey of others even as they are part of the strengthening of your journey.

Organizational thinking must change. For one thing, the emphasis we place on position and title. For some time now, servant leadership has become the en vogue term. Servant leadership sometimes gets interpreted as the way up is down! That sounds right, but the heart motivation is often emphasizing the way up. Seeking to rise in the organization comes from the spirit of competition. OK, if the way to get to the top is to go low, I can do the "go low" thing until leadership recognizes my gifts. Jesus said if you want to be great in the kingdom, become a servant. There are a couple of things I see here. First, this is talking about becoming great in the kingdom. It doesn't have anything to do with becoming recognized in an organization. If you give a thirsty person a drink of water in His name, all of heaven sees it and rejoices. What have we done with this concept? We have changed it to fit into our structure, calling it servant leadership. Jesus said to become a servant, not become a servant leader.

I will have more to say in chapter 14. Becoming a servant is a learning process. I must learn to become a servant. It isn't in the mindset of most people. It takes knowing and being comfortable in your anointing. Your anointing is unique to you and, therefore, cannot be compared to anyone else. From our earliest age, we are encouraged to excel. Put forth our best effort. Become good at something. All our effort goes into becoming someone that others want to emulate or are proud of. Becoming a servant isn't even in the top one hundred on that list.

John the Baptist had the heart of a servant. "I must decrease so that He can increase." John was the older cousin of Jesus. Born into the home of Zechariah and Elizabeth, both of whom were in the priestly line. John, therefore, had every right to take his place in the temple as a priest. Where do we find him? We see John at the Jordan River baptizing and preaching a message of repentance. Declaring that he was simply; "a voice in the wilderness, preparing the way of the Lord." The preparation to enter the priesthood led him to see things differently. It wasn't for Him to serve at the altar but to go out into the wilderness and lift his voice. He heard from his mother as she told how he leapt in her womb when Mary, pregnant with Jesus, visited her. His studies caused him to be astutely aware of the messianic prophecies concerning his cousin, Jesus. The servant John used who he was and what he had learned to take the posture of a servant. Not so he could one day become a leader. Faithful servants serve because they are servants. All we have come to know through study and observation, and all we are through the gifting of the Holy Spirit prepares us to serve.

One Sunday, I invited my son, a missionary, to share with the church I was pastoring. His message was about the calling of the disciples by Jesus. He shared that a young man would only advance from his Torah studies to higher learning if he excelled. Most would return home and begin learning their family's business. Those who excelled in secondary education had an opportunity to seek a rabbi and request to follow him. Many of the disciples were young men who were working in their father's business. They weren't at the top of the class. They didn't seek out a rabbi to follow. Their opportunity to excel in their community was behind them. It was Jesus who sought them. It was Jesus who said to them, "Follow me." No wonder they immediately left their father's business to follow him.

Not long after the calling of the twelve disciples, the spirit of competition manifest. The essence of competition is always present whenever we seek to be more than a servant. Jesus told them that it was the rulers of this world who exercised authority over people, but it would not be true of them. They would become servants of all. They had to learn that it wasn't the heart of a servant to call down fire from heaven on someone who didn't show them the respect they felt they deserved. Jesus said, "I didn't come to destroy men but to save them." They had to learn that they can't buddy up to Jesus and get a better position in the kingdom. The kingdom doesn't work that way. And they had to learn that what Jesus said would be the future of one didn't affect the other. Jesus's call to each one was the same: follow Him.

I was talking to a friend some time back. He had just returned from a weekend meeting with a group to pray over an upcoming gathering of saints. Many of those in attendance were who we would consider senior citizens. Some would be recognized in ministry within their circles but not necessarily widely known. Some in attendance were much younger, with the youngest being fifteen. My friend said the Lord impressed on him that he needed to wash the feet of the fifteen-year-old. Washing the feet of the youngest one is what it looks like to be a servant. Not because it shows how humble you are. Not because, as a leader, you are creating a teaching moment. You wash feet just because the Lord placed it on your heart to do so.

Shortly after graduating from high school, I attended Bible college. I wouldn't say everyone who goes to Bible school thinks they will be the most outstanding pastor or evangelist known. Many I have met would have to admit those thoughts come up from time to time as part of the process of discovering one's God-ordained destiny. If we are the ones responsible for building the church, then the desire to excel is noble. If God is the one who is establishing the church, we must ask ourselves, "How is He doing, and how is He doing it?" Our responsibility is to follow and serve. A current trend in many Christian circles is to have your God-given identity and destiny established. In doing that, we ask questions like "Who did God create me to be? Where will my future take me? What is the call on my life?" All too often, the motivation behind that is a desire for recognition and perhaps even greatness. We look around at others with similar callings and ask how we measure up to them. Scripture teaches us that those who compare themselves among themselves are unwise.

I read in the scriptures that He is taking individual people whom He calls living stones and is "fitting them together into a holy habitation for Himself." Living stones joined together; this is not the model of most churches I've observed. Being joined together implies that there is a process going on in all of us to fit together. Joining together isn't about one leading and the other following. As I read it, I see all surrendering to God's work of transformation. A process that wears off areas that would not allow us to fit together. It implies that at the beginning of the process, we didn't exactly fit together. What is that process? Often, it is adjustments to the attitudes of the heart and our core values. Where He places us in His family is up to Him. How He works on us to fit us together is based on the anointing He placed in us. Deciding which group you want to join or meeting you wish to attend misses recognizing who God is putting in your life and seldom allows the fitting together process.

The first attitude that has to go is that you are not the center of the universe. Most people don't think they have this attitude. Deep down at the core of our belief system, this is a primary motivating belief. We place value on people and other things by how they are affecting me. The core motivation of a servant is "What has God placed in me that I can draw from to make another's life better?" To interpret the New Testament by how it applies to me personally is to miss the broader picture. We are individuals in an entire spiritual community. Not just the local assembly we choose to join. We are individuals in the whole body of Christ, His church. His church exists in heaven and on earth. The church reaches out to time, past and future, to include all who name Christ. To limit scripture to its application to you personally without seeing its application to the whole body of Christ is to miss the intent of scripture. Finding your part as an individual member of the entire body is to find your destiny. Think about a thousand-piece puzzle. Each piece connects to three or four pieces, but the individual is an essential part of the whole by being in their proper place.

> Philippians 2:3–8
> Let nothing be done through selfish ambition or conceit, but in lowliness of mind let each esteem others better than himself. Let each of you look out not only for his own interests, but also for the interests of others. Let this mind be in you which was also in Christ Jesus, who, being in the form of God, did not consider it robbery to be equal with God, but made Himself of no reputation, taking the form of a bondservant, and coming in the likeness of men. And being found in appearance as a man, He humbled Himself and became obedient to the point of death, even the death of the cross.

The challenge here is to become a servant. True servanthood is a learning process. Being a servant is not a natural tendency because servanthood is a virtue of kingdom living. All of life has taught us that we need to stand up or look out for ourselves. The kingdom value of servanthood honestly does look out for the interest of others, placing them above our own. As individual members of a community, serving others with a desire to see them succeed comes back to us in greater measure. As we serve, we receive the fruit of others who desire to see us succeed. As I said earlier, it is a learning process and one that does not necessarily come easy. I don't want to appear to be weak. I don't want people to take advantage of me. I don't want people to think I'm not capable of taking care of myself. I don't even want people to think I need them. All these are fortifying thoughts designed to mask the "I am the center of the universe" core belief. In other words, how will others perceive me if I set about trying to serve everyone else?

Becoming a servant of all is not something we do; it is something we become. It is something we learn as a result of a process. It is an attitude that guides our actions, not a series of activities that proves our ability to manifest a kingdom principle.

Becoming a servant requires us to press into our life as kingdom people.

> John 15:5
> I am the vine, you are the branches; he who abides in
> Me and I in him, he bears much fruit, for apart from Me
> you can do nothing. Apart from Me you can do nothing.

Weakness isn't the position we want to hold. We want to believe that we are fully capable of accomplishing some level of greatness. We are great but not in our ability, and greatness might not look like what the world calls greatness. Who is the one who became the servant of all? Who is the one who emptied Himself and took on the form of a servant? Jesus Christ chooses to take up residence in you. Christ in us is not an insignificant thing or religious terminology. The indwelling of Christ is a living reality and one that, for a kingdom person, becomes the very source of all that they do.

The more we draw on the reality that Christ is living in us, desiring to manifest His life through us, the more we learn the ways of Jesus. As He manifests His life through me, I begin to learn the ways of servanthood. I start to see the fruit in others' lives and see a transformation in my attitude toward others.

Unity is not so much something I'm called to devote my efforts to bring about, as much as joining with Jesus's prayer Father make them one. As Jesus is responsible for building the church, it is the Father's work to make us one. The walls we've built without doors push that unity further away. All the efforts we attempt to bring about our ideas of unity are futile at best. What if we just heard the simple words of Jesus? I am the door. In Him, we find the way to enter true fellowship with those from whom we remain walled off. As we become servants, and as we go through the door of humility, not holding onto our position, we find the way to true fellowship.

Humility is the key. Humbling myself allows me to hear the other person genuinely. Humility allows me to serve others. Truly listening to the heart of what another person is saying will enable us to serve them. It is in the spirit of humility and servanthood that we see the walls come down.

12

Altered Paradigms

IN THE ORGANIZATION WHERE I SERVED AS A PASTOR FOR TWENTY-PLUS years, leaders of congregations were encouraged to write out a five-year plan. I spent a long time thinking about where I wanted my church to be in the next five years. The plan I ultimately came up with was as complete as I could envision. I began setting dates and measurable goals that would guarantee I would fulfill everything written. Somewhere in the process, I realized I was not meeting those quantifiable goals. I began earnestly asking how to receive a vision for my church that I can know is from God. As always, the answer surprised me. I thought that a good leader received directly from God a vision explicitly designed for their fellowship. God would then bring gifted people who would buy into the leader's overall mission. As the congregation faithfully carries out its calling, God's blessing would expand its favor in the community. The impact on the region would attract even more to join and lend their time, talent, and treasure to accomplish the goals and direction of the church. I was also aware of more traditional groups that established their vision by committee and majority vote. Voting on a God-given mandate was foreign to me. I knew that wasn't how I would proceed.

The answer I heard from the Spirit about receiving a vision from God was one I had never considered or seen in practice. First, as a leader, get to know each person enough to know their gifting, calling, and passions. Take each of these and list them. Then you will see the vision God has on His heart for your church. I heard God say, "I don't waste My resources." In that statement, I came to understand that people are God's resources. He brings His resources together so that in giving who they are, the spiritual community fulfills the purposes of God. Each contributing member expands and establishes the vision of every functioning part. To not allow people to function in their gift is to waste God's resources.

If the emphasis is on balancing every word, this would be a place where one might try to bring balance. If we did what everyone wants, we would have chaos. We can't possibly support everyone's vision. The human reasoning of how to stay balanced in our approach is never-ending. Let's examine the idea of each one's passion becoming part of the overall vision. What could that mean? The God-given passion of a person's heart is not the same as the demands for programs designed to meet organizational needs. The demand for programs is often self-centered. An example might be "I want the church where I attend to have a top-notch youth group because I'm trying to keep my teenagers interested in church." An example of a God-given passion might be "I have a heart for youth, so I want to find a way to reach them to serve the whole community."

I began my adult Christian life as a part of a communal ministry that was part of the Jesus People Movement. We had several businesses that supported the residents. One day, the leader shared with several ministers how he decided to start certain businesses, using this example. A young man came to him with an idea for a new business. In his presentation, he laid out a compelling argument regarding the benefits. The leader asked two sets of questions. First was this: "What is your commitment? Do you plan to stay and manage the company until it successfully contributes to the organization?" When the young man said yes, the leader asked the second question. "What ideas do you have on financially underwriting the business until it is making a profit?" A person with a God-given passion is not afraid of these questions.

Many people whose only experience is attending a structured gathering with its various programs have a list of things they think the organization should be doing. They don't want to manage them and maybe don't even want to be involved. They believe the church should do whatever it is they want. They also don't want to finance their ideas. They think that the church should financially sponsor everything. Imagine the drain on the resources of the church if they tried to finance everything everyone wants.

One of the areas that seem to be a huge sore spot in most congregational gatherings is the children's ministry. Everyone wants to be in the central meeting. Parents want a break from their children, even if it's only for an hour. It is almost a surety that the spirit of manipulation will present itself. Those with children place pressure on leaders to provide something for the children. Under pressure to develop something for the children, the result is often duty, not ministry. Because of the pressure to offer programs that meet the congregation's various needs, leaders' resort to methods of intimidation and manipulation to get people to serve. Manipulation, control, and intimidation often are used to fill many of the programs of the church.

I used to do a skit in which I would play the role of the pastor. I have a very discerning look on my face. Placing my hand on my chin with my index finger lifted in front of my mouth, I'd begin to speak in a soft and compassionate voice.

> You know, brother or sister _____, I appreciate you sharing your heart with me. That's a beautiful vision you just laid out, and I can see you have a real burden to bring it to pass. I want to support you fully; I'd love to see that for you. Right now though, it doesn't fit with the overall vision of this church. In the meantime, if you could wait on the Lord's timing and get behind ours, I can see it in your future. Perhaps now you could give yourself to serving our children in our children's program.

Success comes when a ministry results from a vision, passion, gifting, and personal commitment.

A person with a God-given passion will find ways to fulfill their desire. If they are brought together with others, they too can become part of fulfilling the dream. As each one's vision is in the process of fulfillment, the group's effect in the broader community expands.

Before becoming a church leader, I had been in many conversations about what I would do when I was in charge. They all started similarly: "When I become a leader, I'll do or never do …" It's so easy to voice what you'd do if you had unlimited time and money. It's easy to say what you'd do if you've never been in the place of making decisions. If you put yourself in the position of deciding the when and how of each new endeavor, and you are facing the cost of launching that new project, it truly is a different scenario. Suppose there is no one with the passion willing to make the necessary commitment. In that case, the cost in time and treasure will always be higher than you planned for, and manipulation is often unavoidable.

Sometime after my "walk away" experience, I began having convicting thoughts that something was wrong with the whole concept of church being the settling for a one- to two-hour meeting once a week, with its order of service, the limited number of participants, and the congregation sitting as spectators. I couldn't find examples of that kind of meeting, leadership style, or lack of participation by the majority anywhere in scripture. I found quite the opposite.

I have many friends who have focused on the downside of congregational gatherings. The result, and I have been guilty of both attempts, is to campaign against the institutional church (IC). The second is to try to change it. Both rely on human effort. I would suggest taking a more relaxed approach. Allow the Holy Spirit to reveal who God has knit with you. Don't concern yourself with whether they are in an institutional church or not. Joining a group is not the issue; the relationship is. If it turns out that a circle of your friends chooses to begin meeting together, don't resist it. Let your resistance be in the natural tendency to become institutionalized. Keep it free-flowing and relational. Allow everyone to have a voice at the table.

I shared with a few friends who agreed with me. There appeared to be something missing, but they didn't know what. I wasn't comfortable accepting that we couldn't do anything because we didn't know what to do. I began looking for ways to fellowship with other believers in a manner more in line with what I saw in the New Testament. By that, I don't mean just break up into smaller groups and meet in houses. I had seen others attempt that with no real change in the way they met. I wanted to be comfortable with and help others become comfortable with allowing the Holy Spirit liberty in their times of fellowship. I live in a reasonably small town. It is therefore not unusual to see friends almost every time I go out. If I see those meetings as opportunities to encourage each other in the Lord, isn't that being the church? Today I would say yes, but that's not all to be the church Jesus said He would build.

If you are in an institutional church, I'm not telling you to get out. I am suggesting you seek God for His wisdom. Are there some there with whom God has knit you together? If so, can you begin exploring with them why? Together, can you look around and see if others are also desiring a Spirit-led relationship with you? I have seen the life of organic groups formed through friendships grow until they influenced the entire congregation, creating a genuine hunger for something more than a weekly meeting. It can exist even among an institutional church.

I process verbally. I have learned that verbal processing is not always a good thing. During the years I was attempting to find the most biblical way to be the church, I gave voice to many things I wished I would have kept to myself, especially as friends began accusing me of getting too far out there. Others told me they thought I was on a campaign against the church. For some time, I suspect I was. The most substantial opposition came during those years. Friends told me they were genuinely concerned. They believed I was backsliding and preaching things that would lead people astray. That's the last thing I ever wanted to do.

Fear of teaching heresy was another reason I gave the Holy Spirit everything I had ever been taught and asked Him to retrain me according to His kingdom truths. The New Testament was coming alive. I saw things I never saw before. Jesus, a rabbi, taught in the temple as well as in the synagogue. That wasn't the only place He ministered. I didn't see that as His primary place of ministry at all. Jesus taught on mountainsides, on the seashores, in the town square, and at the well. You could see Him ministering in the streets and paths of the city, in a Pharisee's or tax collector's home, etc. Wherever people were, there He was.

Why had I spent so much of my life trying to make a once-a-week meeting entertaining for a few select people? Why had I allowed myself to feel like anything outside of the activities surrounding that weekly meeting was an intrusion?

In the life of Jesus, I saw an ability to have an answer for everyone who came to Him, a response that reached their heart. Not once did the answer sound like a carefully construed religious answer. I saw in Jesus a person who was unaffected by the national sins. Sin wasn't a deterrent at all to His mission of reaching the hearts of the people He came to serve.

I began to be highly interested in the kingdom. No one I knew was talking about the kingdom at the time. I understood that Jesus freely gave the kingdom to us. I soon learned that we are seated in heavenly places together in Him. That meant that we too are far above principalities and powers. Understanding a defeated enemy and all power and authority belonging to the Lord expanded my thinking. All means all. I found myself a part of an exceedingly small number of forerunners—men and women who were declaring a truth that seemed to be a bit before its time.

All of creation is waiting for the manifestation of the sons of God. When the firstborn among many brethren, the only begotten Son, walked the earth, He exercised the power that was His due to the fullness of the Godhead dwelling in Him. The same fullness dwells in His body today. He is the one who said greater works we would do. We seem to be content to drink from the swamp of religion, not knowing that we are dying of thirst.

In Ezekiel, the river of God flowed from the temple. In the New Covenant, the river of God flows out from our innermost being. The body of Christ, His church, is the temple from which the river of life flows.

For the individual to fully understand the church as His body, there needs to be a significant paradigm shift. Words like *assembly, vision,* and even *leadership* need to shift from the idea of corporate meeting times and locations to a more organic interpretation. Let's begin with the concept of assembly, the true meaning of the word *ecclesia*. The Lord said He would build His ecclesia. How is He doing that?

I began thinking about sermons I had heard as well as many I had given. The focus was more on our personal relationship with the Lord than on the fullness of Christ dwelling in His body. Why do we seem to be so focused on a personal relationship when scripture talks about the body? Consider for a moment the following scriptures:

> Philippians 2:3–4
> Let nothing be done through selfish ambition or conceit, but in lowliness of mind let each esteem others better than himself. Let each of you look out not only for his own interests, but also for the interest of others.

> Second Corinthians 5:16–17
> Therefore, from now on, we regard no one according to the flesh. Even though we have known Christ according to the flesh, yet now we know Him thus no longer. Therefore, if anyone is in Christ, he is a new creation; old things have passed away; behold, all things have become new.

It seemed the more I gave myself to this line of thinking, the more I saw the importance of the body of Christ fully functioning, not just holding formal meetings. Although what I saw could happen in a congregational setting, it was much more than meetings could provide. It was about the fullness of Christ in us, His body. As I open my heart to assemble with others in a manner that allows me to get to know them after the Spirit, we are both enriched as we see a bit more of the indwelling Christ.

I already know the fullness of Christ living in me; as wonderful as that might be, it is not the fullness of Christ. If it were, I wouldn't need anyone or anything else. The fullness of what I know, as satisfying to my Christian life as that knowledge might be, still is only seeing in part. It is not the fullness of understanding the mysteries of the kingdom. True kingdom fellowship is individual members of His body being knitted together through the work of the Holy Spirit.

Limiting the extent of coming together to meeting a few times a week with the same people in a congregational setting leaves little room for seeing the function of the individual parts. In congregational settings, the extent of the vision for assembling focuses primarily on the meeting with its prescribed order of service.

Manifesting the unity of Christ's church will not be accomplished through the vision of one man or even a group of people collectively. According to His wisdom and will, the church Jesus said He is building will only be achieved through Christ fitting us together with others as He wills. It becomes our responsibility to seek to know those Christ joins us together with after the Spirit.

Knowing after the Spirit goes well beyond knowing what others believe about certain practices or interpreting certain scriptures. This fitting together is more than attending meetings with those who accept a similar interpretation of scriptures and worship styles. As we allow ourselves to embrace the Holy Spirit's fitting together, we find ourselves stretched. The Holy Spirit seems to be working to bring us into a relationship with believers who do not see things the same way we do. We miss a great opportunity to grow in the Spirit when we walk away from those connections. These uncomfortable relationships become a different interpretation from what I've had in the past of iron sharpening iron.

Seeking to know those with whom I had little in common became part of my stretching. I had to accept that structure, or lack thereof, had little to do with the makeup of Christ's body and the church He is building. There seems to be a quick answer to those seeking to find or experience what God is doing in building His church. That short answer is getting out of the institutional church. That answer seems simple in word, but for some, it is extremely difficult in practice. Not to stop going to a corporate gathering. That is simple. You just don't go. Like me, however, you will probably experience all the thoughts, fears, and emotions I expressed in earlier chapters. You will share some of the things I call the pain of withdrawal, like not worshiping with others and missing the social connections. If your experience with a corporate gathering has been hurtful, knowing millions have stopped attending anywhere may be all you need to walk away. For you, there may be no turning back and even a sense of relief that now you're finally free from the pain. My intention in writing this book is to say that leaving the structure is not required. Changing our understanding and methodology is.

For nearly fifty years, I have been a Christian leader. I still consider myself one. I just don't do it in front of a congregation. Some years ago, I began to understand that my call is to bring people, and especially those lean sheep, to their shepherd. That shepherd is Jesus, the living word. Their guide is the Holy Spirit. I sincerely believe that the best way to understand the heart and leading of their shepherd, Jesus, is in understanding the Bible. That understanding begins with knowing the times and cultures of the people who wrote scriptures and those to whom they were writing. I believe the heart behind scripture needs to be understood for proper application to our lives today. I've recently been interpreting all New Testament scripture and its application through the lens of love. Not the modern-day interpretation of politically correct love that accepts everyone. Bringing someone to their shepherd requires me to teach them how to hear the Lord for their own life. The challenging question in all relationships is "What does love require?" This paradigm shift draws us to embrace those with whom the Lord fits us. It asks that we get to know each other after the Spirit. Hearing their heart allows us to understand their giftings, anointings, and passion. It is the beginning of seeing Christ ekklesia in a community that is being held together by love.

13

Everything Changes

WWJD? YES, WHAT WOULD JESUS DO? WE SPEND SO MUCH TIME trying to assure ourselves that we are doing it right, whatever it is. Our doctrine is correct; the way we worship is right, and even how we assemble is right. After all, we can point to a few scriptures to prove our point. I know few will argue with this statement: Christ is the head of the church. In practice, it seldom becomes a reality. The church is His idea. Man did not come up with the idea of church, and man is not the head. If we want to do it right, we have to allow Jesus to be the head. In doing that, we may want to see if the Bible gives us any indication of how He intends to build His church.

As I look back, I realize this journey of breaking with religious bondage started long before my "walk away" experience. Through visions and dreams and discussions with the Lord, He has been drawing me down this path. I have had times I wished I could bury my head in the religious sand of my upbringing. Then I remember how limited my world would be, and there are so many beautiful people I've become lifelong friends with that I would never have met had I not branched out past the limits of my paradigm.

While serving as a pastor in New York, I began looking into the idea of a house church. After reading several books on the subject, I became convinced that the house church was the biblical way of assembling. As I began looking for successful models, I found very few I would ever want to copy. I've seen a few that appeared more successful, yet there were areas of difficulty even in these.

The house church gatherings I've experienced all closely followed a similar format, believing they were following a biblical mandate to meet in homes. Dozens of books on the subject supported the idea that the house church was the accurate biblical way to meet. What concerned me was the Western culture influencing these house churches. They were no different from a typical church service meeting, except they met in a living room rather than a building. The exact order of service, singing, prayers, sharing, and a message by someone deemed qualified to teach from scripture. Even in groups that promoted relationships, a subtle pressure existed to have someone more learned than the rest who would present a message or lesson for everyone to ponder. Over time the teaching began to dominate, and no longer was it an open group where everyone was free to contribute.

There is a current move to find true ecclesia, a place where we are all necessary and contributing parts of the one body of Christ. Everyone contributing is not easy to do, considering that we all see things differently, even in our interpretation of scripture. Our life experiences, victories and defeats, pain and joy, and our understanding of our vision and purpose are free to be shared with the whole group. These contributions become part of the ongoing conversation. Some advocate that an open meeting means that each person's contribution has equal value. No one is above another in a rank or ruling manner. No one is in charge, and no one is an anointed teacher. I agree with the concept of an open meeting allowing each member to have a voice. Giving equal weight to every voice will eventually break down the very unity it seeks to create. The Bible is clear to bring out that there are gifts of leadership in the body of Christ. Elders and other ministers are appointed. In John's writings, he addresses three groups of people. Those he calls little children. Others he calls young men. Finally, he addresses the fathers. When we attempt to make every voice equal, we limit the value of every person being able to contribute who they are in God. An open meeting makes room for every person to acknowledge the difference in giftings and maturity.

Acts 2:42–47

And they continued steadfastly in the apostles' doctrine and fellowship, in the breaking of bread, and in prayers. Then fear came upon every soul, and many signs were done through the apostles. Now all who believed were together, and had all things in common, and sold their possessions and goods, and divided them among all, as anyone had need. So continuing daily with one accord in the temple, and breaking bread from house to house, they ate their food with gladness and simplicity of heart, praising God and having favor with all the people. And the Lord added to the church, daily those who were being saved.

There's a lot more in this portion of scripture than just a mandate to meet in houses. It appears as if there's room for both house church and temple worship in a more detailed look. I believe this was a much more fluid way of coming together than the assigned home, a prescribed time to start and end the meeting, with its order of service we presently call house church. They went from house to house eating their food with gladness and simplicity of heart, daily with one accord. The phrase *house to house* is one reason why I believe that we cannot look at a portion of scripture and make it a mandate that fits our existing paradigm. Nonetheless, let's see if we can take away from this portion of scripture something applicable. I believe this is more an issue of the heart than it is a methodology.

Some of the concepts that take on significance would be that they ate together with gladness and simplicity of heart. Shared meals were part of this new community of believers. Later, Paul had to instruct the believers in Corinth that they had gotten away from the heart of the shared meal. Those with means would bring a feast and allow those without to go hungry. Shared meals go back to another application that we see in scripture. Those who believed were together and had all things in common. A community that serves the least among them is the visible sign of Christ's church. Love does not seek its own because it esteems others as more important than themselves. Going from house to house appears to be more than a regular meeting. I don't see it as a meeting at all. I see a community of caring people who went from house to house for fellowship and connection.

As they went, they continued in the apostles' doctrine. We have translated *doctrine* to mean "teaching." Here I don't think it was doctrine as much as it was a lifestyle. Indeed, the apostles taught it, but to continue steadfastly is a lifestyle that comes from teaching. That teaching and lifestyle are seen in their unity, gladness, simplicity of heart, and having all things in common. It is the new commandment that Jesus gave in the upper room, "That you love each other, as I have loved you." If our heart truly is to find a more biblical way to be the body of Christ together, we first need to stop thinking about conducting meetings. How does "love each other as I have loved you" practically apply in a markedly different world than the first-century church? How can we manifest the heart of having all things in common? Can we practice the spirit of going from house to house for fellowship, breaking bread, and daily prayers?

Consider the first-century church and its practices. Beginning with Jesus, where do we find Him at eight days, forty days, and again at twelve years of age? In the temple, and why? Joseph and Mary brought Him, according to the custom of a Jewish family of the day. At eight days old, Jesus's circumcision. At forty days after Mary's purification, Jesus was brought to the temple to be presented to the Lord. Today we call this a dedication service. Also, according to Moses's law, Joseph and Mary would have brought the required sacrifice. It was at this time that both Simeon and Anna blessed and prophesied over Jesus. We read about Jesus once again in the temple at the age of twelve. Why? His parents, devout Jews, made their three-day annual pilgrimage to Jerusalem. On their journey home, they discovered that Jesus was not with them. A day's journey back to Jerusalem, a second day looking for him, and on the third day, they discovered Jesus in the temple sitting with the teachers, listening to them, and asking questions.

As an adult, what relationship did Jesus have with the temple? Mark 12:41 tells the story of the widow's mite. It begins by stating that Jesus was sitting opposite of the treasury. Three sections make up the inner court. The court of the priest, which consisted of the temple and the altar. The court of Israel, and the women's court. The treasury was in the women's court, just past the court of the Gentiles and just inside the beautiful gate. Jesus daily taught from within the temple in the court of Israel or the inner court. See Mark 14:49. The temple court was the area that the scribes, Pharisees, and priests frequented. Another place He taught from was Solomon's porch. In John 10:23, Jesus is confronted by many Jews asking Him to proclaim if He is the Messiah. Jesus cleansing the temple was in the court of the Gentiles. It appears from scripture that Jesus spent a considerable amount of time in the temple. Many of the miracles He performed were on the temple grounds, in one court or the other. Finally, Luke 21:37 says that He taught in the temple in the morning and went out to the Mount of Olives in the evening.

Jesus taught in the temple in Jerusalem and the synagogues throughout Galilee (Matthew 4:23). It was in the synagogue in Nazareth that Jesus read from the scroll of Isaiah. "The Spirit of the Lord is upon me because He has anointed me." Synagogues were houses of worship and prayer. Morning, noon, and evening prayers were set to correspond with the times of sacrifice at the temple. Synagogues were also a place of study where teachers and philosophers would debate and give brief lectures after reading from the scrolls. The most sacred item in a synagogue was the Ark, a cabinet that held the scrolls. The synagogue also served as a community center. Synagogues took on a much more significant role for the Jewish community after the temple's destruction in Jerusalem in AD 70. Without the temple, synagogues provided a center for Jewish worship. The word *synagogue* is a Greek word that means "the gathering of the people." Later it came to be known as the place where people assemble. Wherever ten or more came together, they formed a synagogue. Buildings came later. I realized that Jesus, the disciples, Paul, and the believers often met in the synagogue, even to the point of it being their custom.

Let's look at the beginning of the church, which takes place on the day of Pentecost.

Acts 2:5 and 7–11

And there were dwelling in Jerusalem Jews, devout men, from every nation under heaven. Then they were all amazed and marveled, saying to one another, Look are not all these who speak Galileans? And how is it that we hear, each in our own language in which we were born. Parthians and Medes and Elamites, those dwelling in Mesopotamia, Judea and Cappadocia, Pontus, and Asia, Phrygia and Pamphylia, Egypt and parts of Libya adjoining Cyrene, visitors from Rome both Jews and proselytes, Cretans, and Arabs—we hear them speaking in our own tongues the wonderful works of God.

In many metropolitan cities, communities exist around ethnicities, each with its language and culture. Jerusalem was a place where devout Jews of every nation dwelt together. In one day, 3,000 converts representing Jewish people from every ethnicity. Out of every kindred tribe and tongue, the church began. What do you think happened when they got back to their neighborhoods? I realize this is a bit of conjecture, but consider the possibility. What did they know at this point? They knew what Peter had told them in his message, that what they had heard and witnessed was a fulfillment of the prophecy of the prophet Joel.

Jesus's death, burial, resurrection, ascension, and sitting at the Father's right hand all fulfilled King David's words. Finally, that the Messiah they had so long waited for was Jesus and that they had crucified the one God had made both Lord and Christ. Those who gladly received the word and were baptized, Peter said, were now converted. What did they know about being converted? Converted to what?

The follow-up here is that they continued steadfastly in the apostles' doctrine. Love is not something that comes naturally. Interpreting humanism and calling it love can be a natural outworking but is not necessarily the manifestation of Christ's love. Eleven times in the New Testament, John, Peter, and Paul repeated the words of Christ to love one another. In the letter to the church in Corinth, Paul gives a detailed description of what love is. I have concluded that the epistles beginning with Romans and continuing through Jude are the apostles instructing the church in the ways of love.

The concept of appointing apostles did not begin with Jesus. In the ancient Greek world and continuing with the Roman empire, apostles were special emissaries sent with a specific mission. The word *apostle* means "one sent." An apostle was a personal representative of the one who sent them, usually the king. They functioned as his ambassador with his authority and commission to accomplish a specific task. Conquering nations like Greece and Rome used ambassadors to convert newly occupied countries until they looked like their homeland. The intention was when the king visited, they would feel very much at home. Christ, the king, appointed apostles and gave them a charge to make disciples of all nations. Wherever there are communities of believers, the same apostolic doctrine the first believers in Jerusalem heard instructs us. The question is: "Are we continuing steadfast in it?" Are we learning to become a community that the world will say, "See how they love one another"?

Perhaps we need a complete reset. Meeting in a building with a prescribed order of service is not what we should be trying to defend. Breaking away from a corporate structure and meeting in someone's home is not more biblical. Structured versus organic is not the debate. Finding the connections of the Spirit is. While arguing over many nonessentials, those outside Christian circles are not affected by the gospel's message or heart. A paraphrase to 1 Corinthians 13 might be if we figured it all out but have not love, what good is it? What needs to change is how we love.

> First John 3:18
> My little children, let us not love in word or tongue, but in deed and truth.

Love has to become the way we live, not just the words we speak. It is not easy to say, "I love you," and mean it. We usually change it to "I love you, bro," "I love you, sis," or "love ya, man." The word of the apostles to us is that we love each other as Christ loved us.

Romans 12:9–18

Let love be without hypocrisy. Abhor what is evil. Cling to what is good. Be kindly affectionate to one another with brotherly love, in honor giving preference to one another, not lagging in diligence, fervent in spirit, serving the Lord, rejoicing in hope, patient in tribulation, continuing steadfastly in prayer, distributing to the needs of the saints, given to hospitality, bless those who persecute you; bless and do not curse. Rejoice with those who rejoice, and weep with those who weep. Be of the same mind toward one another. Do not set your mind on high things, but associate with the humble. Do not be wise in your own opinion. Repay no one evil for evil. Have regard for good things in the sight of all men. If it is possible, as much as depends on you, live peaceably with all men.

It's time for the Christian community to change. The world is waiting to see the kingdom of God. Love is the only way.

14

A New Breed of Leader

THE DOOR FLEW OPEN WITH A BANG. IN A LOUD, ANGRY VOICE, I HEARD the words "Who's in charge here?" I responded, "The Lord is." I guess that's not what he wanted to hear. With a few profanities, he repeated, "Listen, I want to know who's in charge. I want to talk to him." I stood up and went over to the young man. "If you want to talk to someone, I'll be glad to talk to you, but the answer to your question remains the same. Jesus is in charge here." Why does it seem so hard to understand that concept? What is it about how the church is structured that there has to be a person in charge?

> Psalm 100:3
> Know that the Lord, He is God; it is He who has made us, and not we ourselves; we are His people and the sheep of His pasture.

I don't think I've ever heard a church leader speak of the people they shepherd as the people with whom I am honored to walk. The term I hear most often is *my people* or *my sheep*. I want to ask them, "Are you the one who died for them?" I usually just let it slide. I don't want to get into a long philosophical discussion. This subject of whose sheep they are is anything but semantics with me. It is what I believe constitutes the fundamental paradigm shift that needs to happen. Leadership within Christ's body is a gift and a privilege.

Romans 12:6–9

Having then gifts differing according to the grace that is given to us, let us use them: If prophecy, let us prophesy in proportion to our faith; or ministry let us use it in our ministering; he who teaches in teaching; he who exhorts, in exhortation; he who gives, with liberality; he who leads, with diligence; he who shows mercy, with cheerfulness.

He who leads must do it with diligence. Before I get into that, let me draw your attention to the beginning of this portion of scripture. Having gifts and must do it according to the grace given. Not one of these gifts mentioned relies on the individual's natural ability. Reliance on God is the whole point of the scripture. If they are to lead the way Christ has called them to lead, they must understand that leadership is a gift of grace given to them. Use the gift of leadership, therefore, as an impartation of grace with all diligence.

There was a time when I taught young men who aspired to a position in the church in leadership. Looking back, other than the scriptures I used, I doubt if anything I shared so far would reflect Christ's heart for leaders within His church.

First Thessalonians 5:12–14

And we urge you, brethren, to recognize those who labor among you, and are over you in the Lord and admonish you, and to esteem them very highly in love for their work's sake. Be at peace among yourselves. Now we exhort you, brethren, warn those who are unruly, comfort the fainthearted, uphold the weak, be patient with all.

First Thessalonians was one of the primary scriptures I used to teach on leadership. I was quick to emphasize the latter half of verse 12" those over you in the Lord and admonish you". I would tell them, "You need to know that you are over the people in your charge. It is your responsibility to correct them whenever they need it." Accepting responsibility for another's life is not an altogether wrong interpretation. The word *over* means "to stand before." It also means "to be a protector or guardian." It is not in the interpretation of the word that we miss the heart of Jesus for leaders. It's in the application. Notice the statement "know those who labor among you." Christ's leaders are not just the ones who stand in front during a gathering of believers. They are those who work among the believers. They lead by example, the first ones to get their hands dirty. It's this heart to be among the people as they labor that sets them in the place to be recognized and honored.

> Hebrews 13:17
> Obey those who rule over you, and be submissive, for they watch out for your souls, as those who must give account. Let them do so with joy and not with grief, for that would be unprofitable for you.

In times past, I especially liked this scripture. Mainly because it admonishes believers to obey me while it reinforced my position over them. Additionally, I could justify anything I confronted them with by saying, "I'm just looking out for your soul. You realize I have to give an account for you, and I want to be able to do that with joy." Until I came to the place where I wanted to do things God's way, I refused to accept that this scripture may not be saying that at all. The word *obey* doesn't mean "blind obedience to whatever the person in charge says." It means "to be persuaded; allow yourself to be influenced; to be induced to believe; to have faith." The word *rule* means "to stand before."

Upon further study of this scripture, I discovered that it does not say I have to give an account for you. It does say that as a leader, I have to give account. The report is for how I conducted myself as a leader. Did I exercise my responsibility to those who I labored among with diligence? Did I genuinely watch for their souls, or was I more concerned with demanding respect and submission to my leadership position? Did I lead by example?

Now when I read this scripture, I think of the point man in the military. He goes before the squad while observing the path they're walking on. His responsibility is to diligently look for any danger, pointing it out whenever he sees it. Because they trust the point man, they are persuaded to obey when he says go this way, step over this, or duck below that. The point man is in a place of watching for the lives of those he is appointed to lead. He knows that his position is delegated authority. He has been set in that place and given responsibility for those who follow, which causes him to exercise his leadership with diligence. He does not go off on his own, making demands of others not keeping with the task at hand. At the end of the mission, he reports back to his superiors. His superiors ask about the wounded or those killed in action, giving an account for how it went. With a simple "What happened?" he begins the account. Did he, with diligence, point out the tripwire? Did he spot the movement of enemy combatants just inside the tree line? Did he warn everyone to approach with caution? In a combat zone, the point man cannot guarantee that no one would be injured or killed even if he did his job perfectly. However, the numbers are significantly reduced if he does his job diligently and if those who follow him obey his rulership over them.

> Hebrews 13:7
> Remember those who rule over you, who have spoken
> the word of God to you, whose faith follow, considering
> the outcome of their conduct.

This scripture in Hebrews tells us to remember, which means know, acknowledge, or respect those who rule over you. The writer of Hebrews uses the term "rule over" then explains how they lead. "Know those who have spoken the word of God to you, whose faith, follow, considering the outcome of their conduct". A leader in Christ's church is to be known. They don't just show up to preach or offer counsel. They labor among those they are appointed to lead. They are available to be known; their faith is on display to follow, allowing others to consider their faith-inspired conduct and, by this, persuading others to obey their rule.

Matthew 20:25–28

But Jesus called them to Himself and said, "You know that the rulers of the Gentiles lord it over them, and those who are great exercise authority over them. Yet it shall not be so among you; but whoever desires to become great among you, let him be your servant. And whoever desires to be first among you, let him be your slave- just as the Son of Man did not come to be served, but to serve, and to give His life a ransom for many.

Several years ago, I stopped dutifully reading multiple chapters of the Bible at a time to get through it in a year. I began reading with the intention of understanding, sometimes spending weeks or even months on one scripture. Words like "just as" in Matthew 20:28 are supposed to clarify the statement. Jesus is giving a living example through His own life of the type of servant those who desired to be great should be. I have heard on many occasions from people who held the title of leader say that the reason they were so harsh with someone is that they were serving them. They were watching for their souls. There was a time I understood that reasoning. When I look at the example of Christ's life, I see things like a bruised reed He will not crush and a smoking flax He will not quench.

Second Peter 5:1–4

The elders who are among you I exhort, I who am a fellow elder and a witness of the sufferings of Christ, and also a partaker of the glory that will be revealed: Shepherd the flock of God which is among you, serving as overseers, not by compulsion but willingly, not for dishonest gain but eagerly; nor as being lords over those entrusted to you, but being examples to the flock; and when the Chief Shepherd appears, you will receive the crown of glory that does not fade away.

There are a few things that catch my attention as I read this scripture. Shepherd the flock of God which is among you, *serving* as overseers. The idea of shepherding as an overseer who serves implies a different heart from one who rules over others. Not as being lords over those given into your care reemphasizes this thought. And when the chief shepherd appears, I will receive the crown of glory because "I have been an example to the flock" clarifies giving an account.

It is in my human nature to rule over people. I do not know how to shepherd those I serve. What I have observed and practiced is giving sermons, advice, and direction as needed. Shepherding seems to imply something more. Laboring among those entrusted to me challenges me. It is not in my human nature and therefore causes me to turn to the Lord. Those with whom I walk are His people, the sheep of His pasture.

> Psalm 23:1–6
> The Lord is my shepherd; I shall not want. He makes me to lie down in green pastures; He leads me beside the still waters. He restores my soul; He leads me in the paths of righteousness For His name's sake. Yea, though I walk through the valley of the shadow of death, I will fear no evil; For You are with me; Your rod and Your staff, they comfort me. You prepare a table before me in the presence of my enemies; You anoint my head with oil; My cup runs over. Surely goodness and mercy shall follow me All the days of my life; And I will dwell in the house of the Lord Forever.

If I set my heart to shepherd God's people the way He does, it presents a challenge. I don't believe I can do everything I read in this psalm. If I allow Him to work through me, I can have this same heart toward people. The Lord is their shepherd, I am not, even though according to Peter I am to shepherd people. As one called to shepherd, I should learn how to lead people into a daily trusting relationship with the chief shepherd. In doing so, they too come into a place where they need nothing. As a shepherd, do I know how to make people lie down in green pastures, lead them beside still waters, or restore their souls? As I learn how to point people to the chief shepherd, I provide those things for the ones entrusted to me. Shepherding requires me to know the individual. Knowing them, I can guide them as they learn to trust the Lord in their lives.

This picture of the Lord as shepherd always reminds me of a tranquil painting of sheep grazing in a green pasture next to a quiet stream. That would be nice, but is life always that tranquil? Times arise in people's lives when they need to see an example of someone who has learned to trust the chief shepherd in the middle of the storm. Walking on the waves is the application of leading by example we don't always appreciate. The makeup of Christ's body is many individuals all learning to love one another. Each one learning to love is learning how to come together as one loving community, each individual doing their part. Fitting into a loving and contributing community is not always an easy transition for some. Human fear, suspicion, and wrong motives can cause conflict. The leader has to know how to bring peace into the midst of strife.

I remember one time sitting with a group of church elders. A new pastor had just taken over from the founding leader, who had retired. This leader had a way of working with a wide range of people with differing beliefs and ministries.

The new pastor drew random circles on a blackboard and said, "This is how we've been playing ball, but it isn't going to work like that now." He then erased all the circles and redrew circles in a formation that looked like a football team lined up. He drew the line, halfbacks, fullbacks, and of course, the quarterback. From now on, everyone was going to have a clearly defined position. As the quarterback, he would call the plays, and we would execute accordingly. At the time, it seemed to be a perfectly reasonable plan. After all, he didn't have the same ability to work with people as his predecessor. Today, however, I question that concept. I am beginning to question the idea that being a leader has much to do with directing a local congregation's activities at all.

I do believe there is a time to admonish and even to rebuke someone.

Jesus did it on several occasions. Jesus directed His rebuke in a couple of directions. First, toward those who were ordained to teach the people in the ways of God. It was what they were teaching that led people away from God. They added laws and customs, placing heavy restrictions on people, claiming that they were the requirements of God. Jesus came as the exact representation of the Father. When He came in conflict with those who misrepresented God, He rebuked them for the misrepresentation. Jesus rebuked and even overthrew the tables of those who perverted the house of prayer. Jesus also rebuked His disciples when they resorted to the selfishness of their human desire. Peter saying, "No, Lord, I won't let you do that," when the Lord said He was going to go to the cross and James and John sending their mother to ask the Lord to let them set on His right and left sides in the kingdom are a couple of examples.

Peter and Paul both confronted those who were not acting according to the manifestation of love. Peter dealt with Ananias and Sapphire, who wanted to show they loved the less fortunate, but their motives were selfish and deceitful. Paul dealt with a young man in the fellowship in Corinth who perverted the message of grace by sleeping with his stepmother. Another time Paul rebuked Peter for taking a hypocritical stance when pretending to not be eating non-kosher foods. Christian communities were forming in every city where the gospel had reached. The testimony of these communities would be how they love each other. Leaders took appropriate measures to address anything that did not manifest love, including rebuke or expulsion. In the case of the young man in Corinth, one only has to read the account of 2 Corinthians to see there was a complete restoration when the man repented. Admonishment, correction, rebuke, or expulsion is never from the leader's selfish motivation. It is easy to allow personal irritations to become the source of a leader's counsel or instruction. Correction is always with the heart of restoration. It is always in the spirit of being a representative of the chief shepherd. To manifest the nature of Christ is to esteem others higher than ourselves.

In the seventies and eighties, the corporate world was experiencing a radical change. Top-down or hierarchical leadership styles were giving place to something called servant leadership. Robert K. Greenleaf, the founder of the servant leadership movement while working for AT&T, concluded that most corporations' leadership style with an authoritative head was not working. Retiring in 1964, he founded the Greenleaf Center for Servant Leadership. In 1970 his first essay, entitled "The Servant as Leader," was published. The following are two of what I consider to be the main points.

> The servant-leader is a servant first. Becoming a servant-leader begins with the natural feeling that one wants to serve, to serve first. Then conscious choice brings one to aspire to lead. That person is sharply different from the one who is a leader first.
> The difference manifests itself in the care taken by the servant first to make sure that other people's highest priority needs are being served. The best test and the most difficult to administer is this: Do those served grow as persons? Do they, while being served, become healthier; wiser, freer, more autonomous, more likely themselves to become servants?

The heart expressed here represents the heart a leader in Christ's church needs to have. That first: they want to serve. The desire to be a servant does not come naturally; it takes a conversion of our souls. The human nature seen most often in one who aspires to lead is the need to control. The need for control is a common human weakness. It's why we argue so vehemently our position with anyone who holds a different mindset. When the need for power has not surrendered to the desire to serve, manipulation is unavoidable. If the leader needs to be in control, they closely monitor autonomy, freedom, and creativity. They place safeguards so that dependence on the leader remains intact.

We see the heart of a servant leader in the last two questions. "Do those who are being served grow as persons?" "Do they, while being served, become healthier; wiser, freer, more autonomous, more likely to become servants?" Servant leaders place people above accomplishments.

As long as we view Christ's church as an organization centered around meetings and structure, we will promote the leader's rule over the community. Christ's church is a family; it is a community within a community. In the local community of believers, there is a wide variety of natural talents. A servant in a place of leadership equips people to be servants within their spheres of influence. Our instruction is in the ways of love.

> Ephesians 4:11–13
> And He Himself gave some to be apostles, some prophets, some evangelist, and some pastors and teachers, for the equipping of the of the saints for the work of ministry, for the edifying of the body of Christ, till we all come to the unity of the faith and the knowledge of the Son of God, to a perfect man, to the measure of the stature of the fullness of Christ.

> Ephesians 4:15–16
> but, speaking the truth in love may grow up in all things into Him who is the head—Christ—from whom the whole body, joined and knit together by what every joint supplies according to the effective working by which every part does its share, causes growth of the body for edifying of itself in love.

I come from a background that emphasized the operation of the ministries spoken about in Ephesians 4. The restoration of the offices of the church was an understanding that these gifts never ceased, in particular the apostle and prophet and, to a lesser degree, the teacher. There was much debate on whether there were five offices or four, the pastor-teacher being one, not two. Absolute and final authority translocally belonged to those recognized as apostles. Conflict arose on a local level where the pastor previously was the final authority.

As a result of asking questions, I have become a heart man. I look for the heart of the matter rather than the literal application. Ephesians

4 is one such portion of scripture. Like leadership, these are also gifts. The giver of these gifts was Jesus. Hebrews 3:1 says Jesus is the apostle. Matthew 13:57 says Jesus is a prophet. Luke 19:10 says Jesus is the evangelist. First Peter 2:25 says Jesus is the pastor. John 13:13 says Jesus is the teacher.

Each of these gifts is complete in Jesus, the giver. They are the representation not only of His work on earth but of His heart for His church. When we attempt to take what was never ours, we miss out on what is. Scripture says the government would be on His shoulders. When Jesus left this world, He said, "All authority has been given to me." Because of that authority, He told His disciples, "Therefore go." He did not say, "And now I'm giving it to you." We step into areas of ministry because Jesus has all authority, not because we are the authority. I have concluded that the fivefold is not the government of God. When we attempt to make it so, we enter back into the conflict and abuse of past generations.

Jesus, as the complete embodiment of each of these ministry gifts, gave of Himself. An apostle ministers out of the heart of the apostle Jesus. The prophet ministers out of the heart of the prophet Jesus. Ministering from the heart of Jesus is true of the evangelist, pastor, and teacher as well. These are heart gifts for the church, not the establishment of government in an institution. The apostle carries the heart of Jesus for the equipping of the body of Christ. The nature of Jesus, the apostle, is seen in the words of Paul.

> First Corinthians 3:10–11
> According to the grace of God which was given to me, as a wise master builder I have laid the foundation, and another builds on it. But let each one take heed how he builds on it. For no other foundation can anyone lay than that which is laid, which is Jesus Christ.

Paul recognized that his calling as an apostle was according to the grace of God as a gift. That calling was to lay a foundation that others could build on. So many I've observed who take to themselves the title apostle are building structures and organizations with their name on them. These organizations are not a foundation for others to build on. Paul continues to say that there is only one foundation that is Jesus Christ. Apostles who have the apostolic heart of Jesus lay the foundation upon which individuals can build their lives and upon which the Christian community becomes strong together. That foundation is Jesus Himself.

According to God's grace, the prophet who understands their gift knows they minister out of the prophetic heart of Jesus. Theirs is not to draw people to themselves to receive a word. They don't use their gift to direct individuals, churches, or governments. They use their anointing to equip the saints for works of ministry. A prophet who ministers in their gift imparts desire and an ability to hear the inspired word of the Holy Spirit. The testimony of Jesus is the spirit of prophecy.

The evangelist carries the heart of Jesus to seek and to save that which is lost. They understand the heart revealed in John 3:17. God did not send His Son into the world to condemn the world, but that salvation would come through Him. Evangelists who minister with the heart of Jesus, the evangelist, equip others to be a light that reaches out within their spheres of influence with the gospel.

Pastors go after the one when the ninety-nine are safe. Pastors with the heart of Jesus impart the love and care for one another to other believers. Teachers cultivate in the believer a passion for the written word. They equip the body of Christ to draw out of scripture living truths that transform the heart.

This new breed of leaders understands that their ministry is a gift of grace given by God. When leadership within the church is functioning from the heart of Jesus, the chief shepherd, the body of Christ, is thoroughly furnished for every good work.

•

15

Today's the Day

HE SAID, "HIS NAME IS THE DIVIDER, AND HIS MISSION IS TO DESTROY the ministry." I don't generally pay a lot of attention to prophetic words that focus on the works of principalities or powers of evil. I choose to believe that Jesus defeated the works of the devil. The only power demonic principalities have is through the lies that hold people in bondage. This word was a word that should have been taken seriously. Not because it was spoken directly to us as a ministry but because it is a warning that comes from Jesus Himself. I was part of a ministry that began in the late sixties. We were part of the Jesus People Movement that saw many young people brought to faith in Jesus. Within a few years after its inception, we sent teams to establish new ministries. By the mid-eighties', more than eighty teams were launched worldwide. One of the prophetic brothers brought a word that essentially warned us that a principality known as the divider was assigned to destroy the ministry.

> Mark 3:22–25
> And the scribes who came down from Jerusalem said, "He has Beelzebub," and, "By the ruler of the demons He casts out demons." So He called them to Himself and said to them in parables: "How can Satan cast out Satan? If a kingdom is divided against itself, that

kingdom cannot stand. And if a house is divided against
itself, that house cannot stand.

Division within a home, institution, or kingdom is like a cancerous
tumor. It can go undetected for so long that it might be too late to do
anything about it by the time it is visible. Differences in opinions and
ways of interpreting scriptures do not equate to division. The spirit of
division is present when one or more people take the stance that they
are correct and unless you agree, you are wrong. I think one of the
healthiest statements is "Let's agree to disagree, but let's not allow this
to become a point of contention." Agreeing to disagree puts an end to
the spirit of division. Once the nature of division takes root in a person's
heart, it's only a matter of time before the relationship comes to a bitter
end, often filled with much pain.

At the time of the writing of this book, we are in what is being
called a global pandemic. COVID-19 is a present threat to the health
of millions of people around the world. Doctors are divided over what
the science is telling us or, in some instances, not telling us. Politicians
on both sides of the aisle seem to be using the information and the
misinformation to their advantage. The result is not good. I have never
seen a more divided nation than the United States at this time. On
every level, the division has presented itself. Social media is one of the
most effective tools to promote the divide. It is easy to hide behind
the keyboard and spew out harsh words and insults to others deemed
responsible for destroying our nation. Verbal attacks come regarding the
way you voted. If you travel or are socially active without taking every
precaution, including self-quarantining, then you might be accused
of being responsible for killing people. If you wear a mask or don't,
the accusation is you believe a lie. The allegations are endless, and the
division great.

Institutions, wherever people gather, have shut down, opened, and
then shut down again. Churches were closed, and before they could
reopen, new levels of compliance were in place. Some accused the
government of taking our God-given right to freedom of religion away.
There were outcries of persecution for righteousness's sake regarding the

church's gatherings being shut down or controlled. Some went so far as to defy any orders coming from a government agency.

At the same time, some disagree or are angry with government officials exercising authority over church gatherings; others disagree or are mad at church leaders who take an opposing position to government mandates. Division over this pandemic has brought to light the spirit of division growing in the nation and the church.

I have heard some who are of the persuasion that the institutional church is getting in the way of seeing the kingdom of God say, "this is the best thing that could happen. If all the churches get closed down permanently, maybe people will turn to God for His plan." This way of thinking manifests how deep the spirit of division has taken root.

If there was ever a time we need to hear a clear word on moving forward to bring hope, it is now. There is no better time than the present to speak a word that brings healing and restoration to the divisions within the body of Christ.

Jesus prayed for unity for His disciples and those who would believe in Him through their word. That prayer reaches out to us today. His prayer for unity was so that the world might believe. So much energy goes into evangelistic programs to get the world to believe. Jesus made it clear how that would happen. He said that the world would know that we are His disciples by the love we have one for each other. Look at the words of Jesus's prayer.

> John 17:20–23
> I do not pray for these alone, but also for those who will believe in Me through their word; that they all may be one, as You, Father, are in Me, and I in You; that they also may be one in Us, that the world may believe that You sent Me. And the glory which You gave Me I have given them, that they may be one just as We are one: I in them, and You in Me; that they may be made perfect in one, and that the world may know that You have sent Me, and have loved them as You have loved Me.

The unity Jesus is praying to His Father is more than conformity to a set of rules, worship styles, or spiritual practices. Jesus compares this unity to what He has with the Father and the Father with Him. Referring to this oneness, Jesus says He is in the Father and the Father is in Him. The glory He received from the Father of being in complete unity and oneness with God, He was now giving to His disciples so that they can be one in the same way. Unity is not the result of a total agreement; it results from remaining in the glory of Christ's indwelling. It requires us to hold onto a way of seeing other people through the spiritual eyes.

> Second Corinthians 5:16–19
> Therefore, from now on, we regard no one according to the flesh. Even though we have known Christ according to the flesh, yet now we know Him thus no longer. Therefore, if anyone is in Christ, he is a new creation; old things have passed away; behold, all things have become new. Now all things are of God, who has reconciled us to Himself through Jesus Christ, and has given us the ministry of reconciliation, that is, that God was in Christ reconciling the world to Himself, not imputing their trespasses to them, and has committed to us the word of reconciliation.

This scripture has always convicted me. I have a hard time regarding other people in any way other than according to their human nature. Choosing to view another person as a new creation in Christ is to walk in faith toward them. The battle is not to allow the spirit of division to take root in my heart. I find it is so easy to give way to that spirit. I also find that it is so subtle I seldom know when I am giving in to the pressure to draw away from another person because of a wrong assessment of who they are in Christ.

I have spoken for years on how wrong it is that you can leave a church even on good terms and friends who seem so close never again contact you. Just today, I was in a conversation with a pastor whose church I attended for a season. I had ministered there on a few occasions and often spoke on love and being a family. A couple of weeks after speaking with a passion for being family, I felt called to assist a couple who were beginning a new fellowship. I got involved with the new group and allowed months to pass without any contact with the former. I left them confused and wondering about my motive behind all the talk of being family. It is easy to use empty words if we don't have to live up to their meaning. The subject of the family of God is not empty words to me, but unity and family take work, not just words. It requires a commitment to stay in the relationships into which Christ has brought us. When those relationships face challenges over differences, significant or minor, unity is always the highest goal. There is no better time than now! As the saying goes, "If not now, when?"

Paul gives us an insight into the attitude that must be present to maintain the unity of the Spirit in the bond of peace. He refers to it as a calling and encourages us to walk in a manner worthy of that calling.

> Ephesians 4:1–6
> I, therefore, the prisoner of the Lord, beseech you to walk worthy of the calling with which you were called, with all lowliness and gentleness, with longsuffering, bearing with one another in love, endeavoring to keep the unity of the Spirit in the bond of peace. There is one body and one Spirit, just as you were called in one hope of your calling; one Lord, one faith, one baptism; one God and Father of all, who is above all, and through all, and in you all.

The unity of Christ's body is just that. "There is one body and one Spirit. One faith, one baptism, one God and Father of us all." Without knowing it, the world is waiting to see the manifestation of the body of Christ unified. The only hope for our nation and our world is for the church of Jesus Christ to walk in the glory Christ gave to become one. I understand the tendency to hold our ground on the things we believe are best for our nation. Political, economic, social, and moral issues have become so divisive that I sometimes wonder if it is possible to heal. The only hope I see is to choose to regard everyone according to the Spirit that dwells in them.

In the mid 1970's while on a ministry trip to Alaska, a friend asked me what I see for the body of Christ and its future. At the time, we were experiencing rapid growth, many turning to Christ; our nation was healing from the divide over the Vietnam conflict and Watergate. What was a simple question meriting a simple answer became a prophetic moment. I shared how I saw a time coming when conflict would affect every institution in our nation. I saw public accusations broadcast through every medium. At the time, there was no such thing as social media. I saw vicious attacks against anyone who held a difference of opinion about what was best for the institution. As I spoke about the church, I saw a mass exodus as people tired of what they considered apostasy. I saw men teaching doctrines that appeared to tear down long-held foundational beliefs of the church, causing even more division. What I saw in the spirit looked very much like a war zone. Finally, I saw a publication that read, "If apostles exist today, let them come forth and bring healing to the church."

I believe we all see in part and prophesy in part. It has been my experience that our belief system often influences our prophetic insights and conclusions. At the time, our ministry believed that apostolic authority would set everything in order. Nonetheless, the principle remains true. When there is the kind of division and upheaval that tears us apart, a word of healing is needed. We need to remember that to divide the body of Christ is akin to drinking from the bitter waters of a swamp. The river of God's presence is within, bringing life and refreshing. The leaves of the trees are for the healing of the nations. It is our time, and it is our opportunity to shine in the glory of the oneness of Christ's body.

Is Christianity under attack in America? It certainly looks like it. Is it time to fight the powers that are coming against the church? I believe it is, but I also think we must remember who our real enemy is. Paul said we do not wrestle against flesh and blood. Flesh and blood include political parties or politics in general. Our fight is against principalities, powers, and the rulers of the darkness of this age. It is the same rulers who crucified Christ according to First Corinthians 2:8. The one known as the divider is chief among them. I believe that only unity will defeat our enemy, which is the outworking of love. In the first century of the church, Rome heavily persecuted the church. Judaism attempted to crush it, yet the church continued to grow. In AD 70, as an attempt to stamp out Christianity and Judaism, the temple in Jerusalem was destroyed. Yet the church continued to grow. The more Rome came against the church, the more the church came together in love. If we are under attack and the rulers of the darkness of this age have an assignment to destroy Christianity, we owe the world the victory that is already ours. Let's not fool ourselves; we are in a battle.

It's not a precisely fitting example, but I remember the story of the boy walking on the beach. There were thousands of starfish washed ashore. He picked up one after another and threw it back into the water. A man commented, "You'll never make a difference; there's too many of them." As the boy threw the one he had in his hand back into the ocean, he said, "I made a difference to that one." You may think the task of bringing hope and healing to our nation is too big of a job. You can never hope to make a difference. Let me assure you in every instance where you choose to manifest Christ's love, you are making a difference in the life of that one. When we set our hearts to find the way of love that produces the unity of the Spirit, we make a difference. I won't suggest that it's going to be easy; it will take a lot of soul searching, together with humility. It will require hearing a word from the Lord to know how to love those firmly set in their opinion of what is right. It is so much easier to assemble with those who have the same persuasions as we do. The challenge set before us is to bring a message that brings unity. The place to begin is with the people with whom you are already in fellowship. Seek to find ways to honor one another. Look at how Paul instructs us.

Romans 12:9–18
Let love be without hypocrisy. Abhor what is evil. Cling
to what is good. Be kindly affectionate to one another

with brotherly love, in honor giving preference to one another; not lagging in diligence, fervent in spirit, serving the Lord; rejoicing in hope, patient in tribulation, continuing steadfastly in prayer; distributing to the needs of the saints, given to hospitality. Bless those who persecute you; bless and do not curse. Rejoice with those who rejoice, and weep with those who weep. Be of the same mind toward one another. Do not set your mind on high things but associate with the humble. Do not be wise in your own opinion. Repay no one evil for evil. Have regard for good things in the sight of all men. If it is possible, as much as depends on you, live peaceably with all men.

"If it is possible, as much as depends on you, live peaceably with all men." In another place, Paul says, "As we have the opportunity, do good to all men especially those of the household of faith" This places the responsibility on us. A question that I ask myself and others is "What does love require?" It is easy to project that off on the other person; it's more challenging to take an honest assessment of your part in the relationship. Perhaps a better way to ask the question is "What does love require of me?" Even at that, I don't think the answer is always as simple as taking some action. Love requires me to take on an entirely different attitude and regard for other believers. I will not enter into arguments and abuse, shaming, and cancel culture prevalent in today's world.

Taking on the attitude that Paul is writing about requires a transformation on a heart level. There is only one way I know how to allow my heart to be changed. It requires a sincere prayer, much like the prayer of David. "Change my heart O God, make it ever true." I have strong feelings about all the issues that have our nation so divided. I realize that so does everyone else. Healing to our country is not going to come without the church offering hope for that healing. That offer of hope has to be a demonstration of unity that is in the Holy Spirit.

16

It Is Written

WHAT IS THE ONLY BIBLICALLY AUTHORIZED MOTORCYCLE? TRIUMPH. It is written, "David's triumph was heard throughout the land." One more. What is the only biblically sanctioned car? Honda Accord. It is written, "They were all in one accord."

There are three categories of the 613 laws: moral, civil, and ceremonial. They are written and preserved in a book that has been handed down throughout the generations. Once only reserved for an elite class of people. Thanks to the invention of the printing press, these laws are made available to the general public. In modern times, they are now available in a myriad of translations and paraphrases. "It is written."

Many believe that together with some of the original 613 laws, we now have what Jesus, the disciples, and Paul added as New Testament laws. Over time, most Christians have ruled out the ceremonial and many of the civil laws befitting another era, region, and culture. The teachings of Jesus as recorded in the gospels remain subject to select interpretation. The process of which teachings of Christ apply is the individual's understanding of "It is written." The writings of Paul are relatively easy to apply selectively by using the filter of era, culture, and to whom Paul was writing. Is that the primary purpose of the Bible? Is that the heart of a loving Father who desires a relationship with us? He sent His Son to restore us into the right relationship with Him. Is my relationship with the Father dependent on mastering the laws contained in a book? Isn't that the point of Jesus coming? For centuries, God's people had tried to keep the law and thereby obtain righteousness. Paul tells us that justification will not come by keeping the law.

> Romans 3:20–21
> Therefore by the deeds of the law no flesh will be justified in His sight, for by the law is the knowledge of sin. But now, the righteousness of God apart from the law is revealed, being witnessed by the Law and the Prophets, even the righteousness of God, through faith in Jesus Christ, to all and on all who believe.

The Holy Bible is the number one best seller of all times, and it is considered a sacred book. The average evangelical will tell you with conviction, "I believe every word in that book." I've even heard people say every word in that book, from the table of contents to maps, is inspired by God.

Here are just a few quotes that I've heard over the years regarding the Bible.

- Read it to be wise, believe it to be safe, and practice it to be holy. It contains light to direct you, food to support you, and comfort to cheer you.
- The Bible contains the mind of God, the state of man, the way of salvation, the doom of sinners, and the happiness of believers. Its doctrines are holy, its precepts are binding, its histories are true, and its decisions are immutable.
- It is the traveler's map, the pilgrim's staff, the pilot's compass, the soldier's sword, and the Christian's charter. Here too, heaven is opened, and the gates of hell are disclosed.
- Christ is its grand subject, our good its design, and the glory of God its end. It should fill the memory, rule the heart, and guide the feet. Read it slowly, frequently, and prayerfully. It is a mine of wealth, a paradise of glory, and a river of pleasure.
- It is given you in life, will be opened at the judgment, and remembered forever. It involves the highest responsibility,

rewards the greatest labor, and will condemn all who trifle with its sacred contents.

Sacred text, the infallible word of God, are words used when referring to the Bible. The BIBLE: basic instructions before leaving earth.

The Bible is the owner's manual. Life at best is hard; we're unprepared for the challenges we face. The Bible is our instruction manual that gives the guidance necessary to get through the hard times. We need the Bible so that we can know God. We need the Bible to teach us what truth is. We need the Bible to understand how to live. We need the Bible to help us find the strength to face the challenges of life.

While it may seem like I'm attacking the Bible, I'm not. I am continuing to ask questions. How is it that one book containing sixty-six books written by at least thirty-five authors is the basis for so much division? I'm not saying the Bible caused the division. What I'm saying is every division between Christian organizations holds out that their beliefs come directly from the Bible. The accusations of one organization against another are that they are wrong. They believe it either isn't in the Bible or a misinterpretation of what the Bible says.

Every atrocity known to man was by people using the Bible as their authority for such acts. You can justify anything you want by scripture. To do so requires taking a select and perhaps obscure scripture out of context. Cults form around select passages taken from the Bible. How is it possible that the same book, which provides comfort, healing, and peace to one, leads another to every kind of evil against his fellow man? One person reading the Bible sees their need for a loving Savior, and another sees an egotistical, angry God ready to punish the slightest transgression?

All of these statements and arguments, to some degree, come out of the mind of human reasoning. As I have heard some say, the Bible is not part of the Holy Trinity. It is not the Father, Son, and Holy Bible. However, you cannot dismiss the Bible as some are prone to do and rely entirely on the inner voice, believing that to be the leading of the Holy Spirit or the living word within our heart.

Second Timothy 3:14–17
But you must continue in the things which you have learned and been assured of, knowing from whom you have learned them, and that from childhood you have known the Holy Scriptures, which are able to make you wise for salvation through faith which is in Christ Jesus. All Scripture is given by inspiration of God, and is profitable for doctrine, for reproof, for correction, for instruction in righteousness, that the man of God might be complete, thoroughly equipped for every good work.

Romans 15:4
For whatever things were written before were written for our learning, that we through the patience and comfort of the Scriptures might have hope.

Second Timothy 2:15
Be diligent to present yourself approved to God, a worker who does not need to be ashamed, rightly dividing the word of truth.

Hebrews 4:12
For the word of God is living and powerful, and sharper than any two-edged sword, piercing even to the division of soul and spirit, and of joints and marrow, and is a discerner of the thoughts and intents of the heart.

Canonizing the scriptures Christians call the Bible began as early as the second century CE, predominately focusing on weaving together the four gospels and the letters of Paul with the law and the prophets. In the fourth century CE, different councils established guidelines in how to treat various Christian texts. However, it was not until the fifth century CE that finalizing the books of the Bible was completed. In the sixteenth century CE, during the Protestant Reformation, fourteen books known as the Apocrypha were removed, leaving us with the sixty-six books we call the Protestant Bible.

The translation of the Bible began much earlier. In the third century BC, Greek was the common language of the Roman Empire. The assimilation of the Israelites was of utmost importance. As a result, most Jewish people grew up speaking Greek, not ancient Hebrew. Greek as the spoken language was especially true among those who lived farther from Israel. The Jewish people esteemed the law and the prophets as being tremendously important. Between the third to second centuries BC, Jewish scholars translated the Hebrew scriptures into Greek. This translation is known as the Septuagint. The word *septuagint* means seventy. King Ptolemy II commissioned seventy-two Jewish scholars—six from each of the twelve tribes of Israel—to this task. In the third century BC, they were translating the Torah. Translating into Greek, the rest of the Hebrew Bible and other deuterocanonical texts took place over the next couple of hundred years. The Septuagint includes all the books found in the Hebrew Old Testament together with the Apocryphal books. The Apocryphal books included some additional books from the original Hebrew and others initially composed in Greek. The common belief is that the Septuagint would have been the scriptures Jesus, the disciples, Paul, and the early church would have read. The Catholic and Orthodox Bibles are the modern translation of the entire Septuagint.

A group of scholars began in the tenth century CE, perhaps even earlier, translating the original Hebrew scriptures precisely as they were initially written. These scholars found fault with the Septuagint for including non-Hebrew writings and straying from the ancient Hebrew. It had become the reality that most Jews no longer knew how to read ancient Hebrew. Ancient Hebrew included no vowels, punctuation, or stress marks. As a result, biblical Hebrew became almost unavailable to the general public. Even more concerning was that the original Hebrew made room for a wide range of interpretive errors. In the ninth century CE, rabbis, confident in both written and oral traditions, began making the Hebrew scriptures more accessible. They started the tedious work of translating the original text in a way that would clarify any ambiguity. The goal was to articulate the Hebrew Bible's punctuation and wording so that those reading would understand it exactly as the rabbis had for centuries past. A group of Masoretes (traditionalists) produced the Masoretic Text. Only those books that were originally written in ancient Hebrew were included. Most English Bibles are the result of this translation.

The question I hear most often regarding the Bible is "With so many translations available, which one is the most accurate?" A second question is similar to the first. "Which translation should I read?" My typical answer is "Whichever one helps you to understand what God is saying to you." Now before you prepare your arguments, let me explain my thinking. All of my life, I had been raised to believe only the 1611 Authorized King James Version was accurate. All other translations and paraphrases are filled with heretical errors. As a result, even today, when quoting scripture, I often quote from King James.

In my early twenties, some of my friends read the American Standard or the Jewish Bible. Some even preferred the Orthodox Bible. In discussions around specific text, it became apparent that different translations read differently; therefore, the conclusions drawn were often different. Differences in interpretations became even more evident as newer translations and paraphrases began to make their way onto the scene. I didn't see these new interpretations as anything but a distraction and a perversion of what I considered the authorized text.

How is it that through the centuries, something as sacred as the original Hebrew text, which reveals the ways of God, could be so misunderstood? With so many translations and paraphrases available, is the Bible even reliable? Sometimes I think it would have been easier if I had never started asking questions. The more I ask, the more questions I seem to have. Fortunately, at least for me, I also have some answers.

Regarding the reliability of scriptures, I think it depends on what you mean by reliability. I realize even that answer is cause for some to begin preparing their arguments. I have friends who must read through the Bible every year. Others believe the Bible has to be interpreted through word studies using the word's original meaning, or your conclusions will be incorrect.

I think of two portions of scripture. When Phillip, the evangelist, was walking on the road between Jerusalem and Gaza, he came upon a eunuch sitting in his chariot reading Isaiah.

> Acts 8:30–31
> So Phillip ran to him, and heard him reading the prophet Isaiah, and said, "Do you understand what you are reading?" ³¹And he said, "How can I, unless someone guides me?" And he asked Phillip to come up and sit with him.

> John 5:39–40
> You search the Scriptures, for in them you think you have eternal life; and these are they which testify of Me, ⁴⁰But you are not willing to come to Me that you may have life.

I have concluded that the Bible is reliable in this regard. It testifies of Christ, it reveals the heart of the Father, but understanding must accompany the reading of scripture. Who understands the scriptures more than the one who authored them? It is impossible to have a conversation with Matthew, John, Isaiah, or Moses. We can, however, have a conversation while reading with the Holy Spirit.

Many years ago, I stopped trying to read my Bible religiously, as in beginning to end, chapter by chapter. You may not be experiencing the same thing I did, but I wasn't getting much out of what I was reading. Most of the time, I absentmindedly read whole portions that didn't make sense to me while fixating on scriptures that proved what I already believed. I didn't appear to be learning of Him as the following scripture implies.

> Matthew 11:27–29
> All things have been delivered to Me by my Father, and no one knows the Son except the Father, nor does anyone know the Father except the Son, and the one

to whom the Son wills to reveal Him. Come to Me, all you who labor and are heavy laden, and I will give you rest. Take My yoke upon you and learn from Me, for I am gentle and lowly in heart, and you will find rest for your souls.

I would stop whenever I came to any portion of scripture that challenged my present understanding. Some parts of scripture are related to the times and customs of the day. These weren't as important to me as other scriptures that spoke of principles of the life God had for me. I determined not to move on until I understood the words I was reading and their application to my life. Over time, I realized that this approach was bringing insights and a transformation into my life. I was no longer just reading ink on paper. I was coming to the author and seeking to understand the meaning of the words I was reading. The Bible was beginning to come alive. I believe even more important than the Bible coming alive was that Jesus was becoming more real to me. The Father was becoming more approachable as I began to know Him. The word was changing my heart.

Reading the Bible without allowing the Holy Spirit to reveal the application leaves the reader trying to understand on a purely rational level. Paul says that we're not able to comprehend spiritual things through our flesh.

> First Corinthians 2:10–11 and 14
> But God has revealed them to us through His Spirit. For the Spirit searches all things, yes, the deep things of God. For what man knows the things of a man except the spirit of the man which is in him? Even so no one knows the things of God except the Spirit of God. But the natural man does not receive the things of the Spirit of God, for they are foolishness to him; nor can he know them for they are spiritually discerned.

Second Peter 1:20–21
knowing this first, that no prophecy of Scripture is of
any private interpretation, for prophecy never came by
the will of man, but holy men of God spoke as they were
move by the Holy Spirit.

Recently I read a meme on Facebook. "If the Bible doesn't lead you
to love more, you should question your understanding of the Bible."
Author unknown. Understanding and godly application from reading
the Bible should result in transformation. I have concluded that I can
pattern my life on the teachings of scripture if I understand a few
guidelines. The first one is that the foundation of my faith is not the
Bible. Here's what Paul had to say in this regard:

Second Corinthians 3:10–11
According to the grace of God, which was given to me,
as a wise master builder I have laid the foundation, and
another builds on it. But let each one take heed how he
builds on it. For no other foundation can anyone lay
than that which is laid, which is Jesus Christ.

Jesus Christ, the living word, is the foundation upon which I build
my life. Whatever I receive from scripture must point me to Jesus. If
it leads me to works, performance, condemnation, or any law-keeping
level, I have strayed away from the heart and the intent of the Bible.

As I conclude this chapter, I want to share a series of questions I ask
when reading scripture.

1. Is this one of my go-to scriptures proving an already firmly held
   religious position? If my answer is yes, I ask an additional set
   of questions.
   a. Has this position brought me to freedom?
   b. Has this position made me more loving?
   c. Am I willing to search out differing positions on the subject?
   d. Am I open to having my position adjusted?

  e. Am I open to doing a word study of the primary words in the text?

  f. Am I open to researching to whom this scripture was written and the manners and customs of the day?

  g. Have I asked the Holy Spirit how the application of this scripture I'm reading will bring me to a clearer understanding of love?

2. If I'm reading and I become aware of arguments or conflicting thoughts in my mind, I make a conscientious effort to stop and ask why.

  a. Why is my heart arguing against what I am reading?

  b. Is it because this is not my experience?

  c. Is it because this is not how I see God, Jesus, or the Holy Spirit?

  d. Is it because this is not how I believe we're supposed to act?

  e. Is it because it goes against everything I've ever been taught and believe?

The purpose of these questions is to get to the root of arguments that come when reading scripture. They reveal what my heart believes. I have learned to be comfortable with exploring the source. In the process of researching, I find the answers. I think the heart of the living word, Jesus, delights in my discoveries.

A couple more questions I ask when reading scripture are these:

3. Is my understanding of what I am reading revealing the heart of Jesus?

4. Is it drawing me to desire a closer relationship with the Lord?

5. Am I discovering the heart of God the Father toward me?

6. Is my understanding of the God of the Bible consistent with the God Jesus came to reveal?

7. Is it clarifying the way of love?

8. Is it applicable to my life?

These last few questions have been of real significance since I stopped reading the Bible as an obligation. As I seek understanding in what I am reading, is understanding bringing me to see Jesus and the Father in ways I've never known them? Am I able to apply any new knowledge I'm receiving to my life that results in becoming a more loving person? The purpose of learning to fellowship with the Lord through the written word is transformation.

> First Timothy 3:16–17
> All scripture is given by inspiration of God, and is profitable for doctrine, for reproof, for correction, for instruction in righteousness, that the man of God may be complete, thoroughly equipped for every good work.

When we receive scripture as it's intended, we can rest in the doctrines found therein. It will reprove and correct wrong beliefs as well as motives. Scripture will instruct in the ways of righteousness. It will equip you for every good work and bring you to a place of being complete in God. This change is personal, but in the transformation of individuals through applying the written word, Christian communities also become transformed. As Christian communities grow in love and the application of the heart of scripture, our world is affected for good.

17

More than Slogans

My usual greeting is "How you doing?" Most of the time, the response is "OK" and perhaps a follow-up "How about you?" I suspect I'd be a bit taken back if someone who wasn't having the best day began telling me how they were really doing. Several years ago, I met a couple with the usual greeting. The woman's response was "Under the spout, too blessed to be stressed." Having been raised in a Pentecostal home, I understood the expression "under the spout." The remainder of the statement is where the glory comes out. I knew the phrase, but I never understood it. Is there a spout where God's glory comes out? If you're under it, you get the blessing of God's glory. If you're anywhere else, you don't. How about that second one? "Too blessed to be stressed." Is that how it works? Does it have to be tied together with being "under the spout"? If you're not under the spout, are you subject to stress?

Several years ago, my wife and I were returning home from spending time with my grandmother. It was early Sunday morning, and I was supposed to speak at our church. As we had a three-hour drive, I left early enough to arrive home with time to spare. An hour into the drive home, I drifted onto the shoulder and hit the guard rail. I overcompensated and threw the car into a spin before it rolled over. The highway patrolman said we skidded upside down seventy-three yards before coming to a stop. A van stopped, and the man put out flares. He then let us sit in his van until the ambulance and highway patrol arrived. I remember looking at our car and seeing a bumper sticker that said, "I have decided to follow Jesus." Later, I wondered how much of a witness that bumper sticker was on a wrecked vehicle upside down in the middle of the highway.

I have seen scores of bumper stickers, T-shirts, church signs, and Facebook memes over my lifetime. I wonder who wrote some of them and what they were thinking. Here's one for you: "I want to be so full of Christ that if a mosquito bites me, it flies away singing; there's power in the blood!" What does that even mean? I get the sentiment, but does anyone believe their veins carry the blood of Christ? Do we ever consider how a non-churched person would interpret that?

Here are a few of my favorites:

- Forecast for tomorrow: God reigns, and the Son shines.
- Skip rope, not church.
- Exercise daily; walk with the Lord.
- The best vitamin for a believer is B1.
- Ketchup with Jesus and relish his love.
- In case of rapture, this car will be unmanned. (This one is my favorite.)

I'm sorry, folks. I don't want to offend anyone, but what kind of witness do these slogans give? I have a hard time believing that these sayings represent the heart of Christ for His church or a solid witness.

One slogan I think most have heard in one way or other is this: "It's not a religion; it's a relationship." I understand why someone would say this. I also know what they are trying to communicate. The statement isn't factually correct. You can argue all you want, but Christianity is a religion. What becomes a witness is when the individual indeed enters a relationship with the living God. A relationship with the living God takes on a life of its own. The union with God has a positive effect on your life. Let's take a closer look at the difference.

It wasn't until I walked away from a corporate gathering and public ministry that I realized how much of a religion Christianity is. Not only that but the bondage that the Christian religion puts on its most devoted followers. That bondage is responsible for keeping people from experiencing the freedom in the relationship the Father intends for us. Religion is the adherence to a list of specific rules. It is the worship of God or the supernatural. It is a commitment or devotion to faith in a deity. You cannot get away from the fact that Christianity is a religion. That fact does not have to have a bad connotation. Let's take a look at the first statement: adherence to a list of religious rules.

> Matthew 19:16–22
> Now behold, one came and said to Him, "Good Teacher, what good thing shall I do that I may have eternal life?" So He said to him, "Why do you call Me good? No one is good but One, that is, God. But if you want to enter into life, keep the commandments." He said to Him, "Which ones?" Jesus said, "'You shall not murder,' 'You shall not commit adultery,' 'You shall not steal,' 'You shall not bear false witness,' 'Honor your father and your mother,' and, 'You shall love your neighbor as yourself.'" The young man said to Him, "All these things I have kept from my youth. What do I still lack?" Jesus said to him, "If you want to be perfect, go, sell what you have and give to the poor, and you will have treasure in heaven; and come, follow Me." But when the young man heard that saying, he went away sorrowful, for he had great possessions.

The first thing that stands out to me is this young man's answer. "All these things I have kept from my youth." Jesus didn't challenge that statement. I believe many devout Jews of the day would have been able to make that statement. The apostle Paul said as much about himself. "Concerning the righteousness which is in the law, blameless." Yet with all the diligence to keep the law, this young man knew something was lacking.

I grew up in a home under our denomination's understanding of holiness. I think it would be easier to list what we could do rather than what we couldn't do. The list of *could dos* is much shorter. Suffice it to say, what we couldn't do was anything a young boy would consider fun. We were not allowed to dance or watch movies in a theater, and TV was taboo when I was an adolescent. Playing games with dice or playing cards was out. Roller skating in a rink was marginal, bowling was OK except on Sunday, and the big one was missing church, even while on vacation.

The last commandment listed in this story by the Lord was "You shall love your neighbor as yourself." I find that interesting for a couple of reasons. First, Jesus didn't say you shall love the Lord God with all your heart, soul, mind, and strength, and you shall love your neighbor as yourself. He only said you shall love your neighbor as yourself. Second that the young man took that in stride, saying, "I've done all of that." When Jesus told His disciples in the upper room, "Love one another as I have loved you," He was placing an entirely new emphasis on love. No longer would you love your neighbor as a fulfillment of the law. No longer would love be interpreted by how you love yourself. Love, as Jesus commanded, requires an ongoing relationship. It goes beyond what humanism recognizes as love. You cannot love as Jesus loved by simply observing a set of rules or lifestyle.

A few years ago, I changed my status on Facebook to "Lover of the Jesus way." I didn't do it for any religious reason. I wasn't trying to be more spiritual or biblically correct. I just came to realize that the term *Christian* didn't describe what I wanted people to know about me. The word *Christian* first came about in Antioch. It was a term used to mock believers. Before they were called Christians, they were simply called "people of the way." They desired to live in the way that Jesus modeled and taught. They understood that there is a way we live that is the way of love. This way is more than following a moral code of conduct or a set of religious rules. Changing my status was a way of stating that I am setting my heart to discover the way of Jesus and walk in it. Originally the term *Christian* was an offhanded compliment. The word *Christian* means "follower of Christ." Those who called believers Christians were testifying that these people are followers of Christ. Today it can mean you have particular leanings morally, politically, or socially. It can also mean that your religious beliefs are different from other religions. It no longer has the clear and definite meaning: follower of Christ.

Every religious group has its set of rules. There's nothing wrong with having rules. When we allow codes of conduct to define a person's level of maturity as a follower of Christ, we have walked away from a relationship and slipped into the bondage of religion.

A person sits in a church meeting wishing they were out enjoying the weather. Church boards spending more time debating paint colors or carpet samples than ways to reach out to their community. Pastors spend more time polishing their weekly sermon than being with people. Some will join campaigns to get local, state, and federal agencies to enact laws that address social injustices, poverty, and prejudice, thinking that in so doing, they are fulfilling some moral obligation. The list of religious activities that Christians involve themselves in without focusing on a vital and growing relationship with the Lord is long.

There is a widely accepted belief system regarding how a relationship with Jesus begins. It starts with hearing the gospel message. In some form or fashion, a person hears the gospel in a way that moves them to respond.

> Romans 10:13–15
> For "whoever calls on the name of the LORD shall be saved." How then shall they call on Him in whom they have not believed? And how shall they believe in Him of whom they have not heard? And how shall they hear without a preacher? And how shall they preach unless they are sent? As it is written: "How beautiful are the feet of those who preach the gospel of peace, who bring glad tidings of good things!"

Contextually speaking, this scripture is not laying out a road map for how to get someone saved. This entire portion of scripture is the apostle Paul sharing his heart for Israel to hear and believe the gospel. What makes the difference between religion and a relationship is the motivation behind our activity. Religion creates formulas to follow.

An example would be no one can get saved without being witnessed to first. Follow the Roman road or the four spiritual laws. If their soil is ready, the seed will bear fruit. Once they've repented of their sin, prayed the sinner's prayer, and invited Jesus into their life, now they're saved. Now they need to get into a good fellowship, read the Bible, and pray every day. This way, they can learn the ways God wants them to live as newborn Christians. If they are faithful in those disciplines, they will grow into mature Christians. That all sounds good and isn't altogether wrong. Without understanding the relationship with Jesus, this practice places a person on a path of legalism and religious performance.

A relationship with the Father, the Son, and the Holy Spirit begins with hearing the gospel of the kingdom. The gospel of the kingdom is so much more than a "fire escape" message. The gospel of the kingdom begins with love. "For God so loved the world that He gave His only begotten Son." Jesus was the exact representation of the Father. If you see Jesus doing or saying it, that is what the Father is doing or saying. The way Jesus expressed love, caring, and compassion is the way the Father loves; He is caring and compassionate. He loved you before you were even born. He gave his life to restore humankind's relationship with the Father. This relationship begins by believing God has always loved you and has always wanted to have a relationship with you.

The relationship God wants to have with you guides you in life to avoid many of the pitfalls resulting from relying on your human understanding. God's desire for you is that you live life to the fullest. He says it this way: "I have come that you might have life, and life more abundantly." Your relationship with God will cause you to grow in your relationship with the Christian community. Your relationship will also guide you through the challenges of involvement with the Christian community without falling into the bondage of religious observances. A community of Jesus followers, lovers of the Jesus way, is made up of individuals who are learning to love each other as Christ loved them. Doing that requires understanding the depth of that love. It also requires knowing the way Christ shows His love.

Spiritual leadership is part of the community, not to control or exercise their authority but to model how to hear the shepherd's voice. Each individual in the community is responsible for hearing the Lord and following His voice. As each member grows in their relationship and contributes to that relationship, the whole community grows together in love. God intends that His family will grow in their relationship with Him as well as numerically. This numerical growth happens as those outside the community see the difference in the lives of the believers. The quality of their love for each other testifies that they are followers of the Jesus way. This love is a genuine expression of God's love for humanity, not merely a humanitarian display of social justice. Growing in a relationship with God requires learning how to hear His voice. Hearing His voice means learning how to pray, interpret the Bible, and listen to the heart's inner voice.

A relationship with God accepts that God is not a distant deity living way off in a spiritual realm. Religion teaches God is in heaven, and if we expect to get anything from Him, we have to learn how to pray just right to get His attention. We also have to be living right, or He probably won't answer our prayers. Don't get me wrong. I'm not saying that God isn't in heaven. First of all, God is omnipresent, meaning He is everywhere. Heaven is His throne. The earth is His footstool. Jesus told us how the relationship begins and how close God is to us.

John 14:23
Jesus answered and said to him, "If anyone loves Me, he will keep My word; and My Father will love him, and We will come to him and make Our home with him.

John 14:15–17
"If you love Me, keep My commandments. And I will pray the Father, and He will give you another Helper, that He may abide with you forever—the Spirit of truth, whom the world cannot receive, because it neither sees Him nor knows Him; but you know Him, for He dwells with you and will be in you."

In these couple of verses, Jesus is sharing the result of love. The Father, the Son, and the Holy Spirit will make their home in you. God's indwelling is much more than religious rhetoric. The reality of God living inside an individual, when realized, becomes the foundation upon which we establish a growing relationship. As individuals, we don't fully realize the impact of this relationship. According to scripture, we are members of one another. To ultimately realize God coming and making His home in us, we must recognize the whole body of Christ. The fullness of the Godhead dwelt bodily in Christ. Now we are the body of Christ and members in particular. To see the fullness of the Godhead, we must see and embrace the fullness of His body, not just certain individual parts. God calls us to experience a growing relationship with Him as a loving Father. The promise of Fatherhood with His whole family is the foundation of our relationship with God.

Hebrews 8:6
But now He has obtained a more excellent ministry, inasmuch as He is also Mediator of a better covenant, which was established on better promises.

2 Peter 1:2–4
Grace and peace be multiplied to you in the knowledge of God and of Jesus our Lord, as His divine power has given to us all things that pertain to life and godliness, through the knowledge of Him who called us by glory and virtue, by which have been given to us exceedingly great and precious promises, that through these you may be partakers of the divine nature, having escaped the corruption that is in the world through lust.

We become a partaker of His nature as we learn to live in the promises of God, not through careful observance of religious practices. This is the relationship God has always desired to have with us. The promises He made are the basis of that relationship. It frees us from having to perform to get God's attention. Learning to live in the promises of God is an exercise of faith. In the beginning, it is foreign to our entire way of thinking. Life's instruction tells us that we have to work hard or fight for something we want. God tells us that our labor is to enter into His rest.

In the scripture above, we see that his divine power gave us (past tense) all things (that leaves nothing out) pertaining to life and godliness. What can you add to that through your attempts to earn anything from God? Jesus invites us to come and learn of Him. He goes on to say, "For I am meek and lowly in heart: and you will find rest for your souls." There it is again. Jesus wants us to be at rest. Another way to say it is Jesus wants us to be at peace. One of His promises is that He will give us peace—His peace. It won't come in the way we strive for peace in the world. Attempting to control everything for a moment of peace won't produce the promise. Ceasing from all our human efforts and receiving through faith that He has already given us His peace is the only way we receive it.

A relationship with God the Father, God the Son, and God the Holy Spirit becomes a living reality when we step out of the bondage of religion. Stepping out of the bondage of religion comes as we realize that being a follower of the Jesus way entails more than slogans. It's more than a careful and diligent observance of religious practices. It is a living and vital relationship based on receiving all the promises our loving Father has freely given us.

18

The Next Step on the Journey

I'VE CONCLUDED THAT LIFE IS A JOURNEY. I'VE SHARED PRETTY OPENLY about my journey so far. Even now, I choose not to stop with what I've learned, lest it become a pool of bitter water cut off from the flow of the river. As long as I have breath in my lungs, the relationship with the Lord moves me forward. I'm not much of a walker; I used to be. In college, I walked all over Portland. If I wanted to go somewhere, I walked. Thinking about walking, it's as simple as putting one foot in front of the other, one step at a time. If you do that consistently, you will eventually get to where you're going. That's a no-brainer. As a follower of Christ, I don't know where my life is going to end up. I have a general idea, and I suspect I know my ultimate destination, but the steps required to finish my journey are unclear. However, there is one who not only knows where my life's journey is taking me but also knows the very next step. I read that He even orders those steps. So it's one foot in front of the other, one step at a time.

They say hindsight's twenty-twenty. I don't know if that true, but I do know one thing. I rarely get it right the first time trying to interpret what God's saying or doing. Looking back over the years, I've been following the Lord; I've adjusted and amended almost everything I believed. Occasionally, I'll share a present understanding, and someone will state, "That's not what I heard you teach in the past."

Many of the things I've shared in this book have gone through the amending and adjusting process. Attempting to apply the promises of God to my life without understanding the body of Christ is one of those things. I have friends and people in my life who, like me, read something in the Bible and, with no regard to setting, culture, or it being in the Old Covenant or New Covenant, or any other parameters, attempt to apply it to their life. If they believe it's a command, they try to live up to the most stringent interpretation. If it's a promise, they claim it as theirs personally.

In 2018, I had an experience with the Lord in which I believe I heard Him say, "I am bringing the body into the experiential knowledge of Christ in you, the hope of glory." I didn't hear any more than that. My takeaway from that impression was Christ is in me fully, so He will bring me into experiencing the fullness of His glory. Since you are a member of His body, that word applies to you; in fact, it applies to everyone who's a member of his body personally. That's not what He said, and that's not what the promise recorded in scripture says. We do that with many of the promises regarding the kingdom of God as well. We attempt to make them fit in their fullness in our lives individually. We see the hope of God's glory because He is in His body. The promise is Christ in you (the body), the hope of glory. If the manifestation of the glory of God is important, the coming together of His body must become essential.

Another promise is it is the Father's good pleasure to give us the kingdom. Yes, but no one individual, or the millions of individuals worldwide, have the whole of the kingdom. The Father takes pleasure in giving the kingdom to the royal priesthood and holy nation.

This idea of the individual being part of the whole body of Christ is so much more than theoretical or spiritual reality. I realize I've said this several ways, but I cannot overstate it. You are only responsible for being connected to those Christ connects you to. It does not require you to join an organization; however, it doesn't prohibit you either if you are so inclined. You connect with those of Christ's choosing; they link with others who are joined together with others still. This is the mystery of Christ's body.

Understanding the body of Christ from the kingdom's perspective goes way beyond the Western or evangelical definition of what it is to be a Christian. Jesus, walking by, some fishermen simply said, "follow me." Immediately they left the nets they were mending and began following Him. Jesus called them disciples. No sinner's prayer, no commitment card, just "Follow me," and they followed. After I started looking for followers of Jesus, I've met many who couldn't tell you the day they got saved, but they can tell you how they have tried to follow Jesus in their life. Perhaps if we were to stop with our religious practices and start walking with those who desire to follow Him, we would discover many more genuine disciples.

John writes in his epistles, "He who loves is born of God because God is love." Additionally, if a man says he loves God but hates his brother, he is a liar, and the truth is not in him. So perhaps you can explain how we can declare a person who doesn't like this person and hates that one but prayed a prayer is a Christian, but someone who genuinely loves others and tries to follow Christ needs to pray the sinner's prayer to get saved. A Samaritan woman, drawing water from a well, has a conversation with Jesus. After the conversation, she invites her whole community to come and see a man who told her everything. She is a woman who has been with five men, and the one she was currently with was not her husband. At least from the record of scripture, she never confessed all her sin and asked Jesus to be her Savior. The closest thing to that was in response to His statement about the water He would give that would quench her thirst; she simply said, "Give me some of this water."

Human effort can only establish a religious system that leaves a bad taste in so many mouths. Perhaps it's time we stop and take another look at how Jesus did things. How did He gather people to Himself? How did the church begin and grow? In a word, love, but let's look a little deeper. He told Nicodemus, "You must be born again." Nicodemus was a Jewish religious leader, who I'm pretty sure was looking forward to the Messiah's coming. I believe he was probably a pretty righteous keeper of the law of Moses. Why did Jesus tell this man he needed to be born again? Religious activity or adherence will not allow us to see the kingdom. A person must be born of the Spirit to inherit the kingdom. It is possible to follow all the rules, observe all the religious practices, and miss the kingdom. Being born again is more than saying a prayer;

it embraces the meaning of the word *repent.* To repent is to change your way of thinking.

> Romans 12:1–2
> I beseech you, therefore, brethren, by the mercies of God, that you present your bodies a living sacrifice, holy, acceptable to God, which is your reasonable service. And do not be conformed to this world, but be transformed by the renewing of your mind, that you may prove what is that good and acceptable and perfect will of God.

Do not be conformed to this world's way of thinking but be transformed by renewing your mind. The renewing of our minds manifests in how closely we follow Jesus. Following Jesus begins and ends with loving each other the way He loves us. Inheriting the kingdom, which comes from being born again, is making a choice. Jesus said it is selling everything to purchase the pearl of great price. Purchasing the field where we found the pearl isn't about immersing ourselves in religious activity until we die or burn out. It's about not being double-minded when it comes to committing to make following Jesus our lifelong commitment. Following Jesus moves us away from the swamp water of tradition and religion to draw from the river of growing intimacy and relationship with the triune God: Father, Son, and Spirit.

I shared the impression I had regarding the hope of glory, being the indwelling of Christ with a friend. His reply was to share with me a series of scriptures and what they were speaking to him. Without drawing any conclusions, I will list them in the order he shared. I invite you to meditate on them and see what the Lord speaks to your heart.

Under the Old Covenant, King David ascribes to the Lord a name.

> Psalm 24:7–10
> Lift up your heads, O you gates! And be lifted up, you everlasting doors! And the King of glory shall come in. Who is this King of glory? The LORD strong and

mighty, The LORD mighty in battle. Lift up your heads, O you gates! Lift up, you everlasting doors! And the King of glory shall come in. Who is this King of glory? The LORD of hosts, He is the King of glory. Selah.

Ephesians 1:15–23
Therefore I also, after I heard of your faith in the Lord Jesus and your love for all the saints, do not cease to give thanks for you, making mention of you in my prayers: that the God of our Lord Jesus Christ, the Father of glory, may give to you the spirit of wisdom and revelation in the knowledge of Him, the eyes of your understanding being enlightened; that you may know what is the hope of His calling, what are the riches of the glory of His inheritance in the saints, and what is the exceeding greatness of His power toward us who believe, according to the working of His mighty power which He worked in Christ when He raised Him from the dead and seated Him at His right hand in the heavenly places, far above all principality and power and might and dominion, and every name that is named, not only in this age but also in that which is to come. And He put all things under His feet, and gave Him to be head over all things to the church, which is His body, the fullness of Him who fills all in all.

Hebrews 2:9–10
But we see Jesus, who was made a little lower than the angels, for the suffering of death crowned with glory and honor, that He, by the grace of God, might taste death for everyone. For it was fitting for Him, for whom are all things and by whom are all things, in bringing many sons to glory, to make the captain of their salvation perfect through sufferings.

Romans 8:15–21

For you did not receive the spirit of bondage again to fear, but you received the Spirit of adoption by whom we cry out, "Abba, Father." The Spirit Himself bears witness with our spirit that we are children of God, and if children, then heirs—heirs of God and joint heirs with Christ, if indeed we suffer with Him, that we may also be glorified together. For I consider that the sufferings of this present time are not worthy to be compared with the glory which shall be revealed in us. For the earnest expectation of the creation eagerly waits for the revealing of the sons of God. For the creation was subjected to futility, not willingly, but because of Him who subjected it in hope; because the creation itself also will be delivered from the bondage of corruption into the glorious liberty of the children of God.

The reality of the triune God—Father, Son, and Spirit—dwelling in His body and the body finding their life, movement, and being in Him is still, for the most part, a mystery. I believe it is a mystery that is soon to be revealed more fully than the body is currently experiencing.

I'll leave you with this: Ask questions, and spend time meditating on the things the Holy Spirit says. Read scripture to gain understanding. Press into and enjoy the relationships the Lord brings to you. Rest in a growing intimate love relationship with the Father of glory.

Enjoy the journey!

Printed in the United States
by Baker & Taylor Publisher Services